Stonewall Inn Editions

Michael Denneny, General E

PROFILES IN GAY & LESBIAN COURAGE

Reverend Troy D. Perry
Thomas L. P. Swicegood

St. Martin's Press   New York

Cover photographs (clockwise from upper left): Leonard Matlovich, Joan O'Leary, Elaine Noble, Gilberto Gerald (Sharon Farmer), Harry Hay (Robert Giard), Barbara Gittings (Kay Lahusen), Harvey Milk (UPI/Bettmann Newsphotos), Ivy Bottini.

Design by Karin Batten

Library of Congress Cataloging-in-Publication Data

Perry, Troy D.
    Profiles in Gay and Lesbian courage / Troy D. Perry
and Thomas L.P. Swicegood.
        p.   cm
    ISBN 0-312-08281-9
    1. Gays—United States—Biography.   2. Lesbians—
United States—Biography.   I. Swicegood, Thomas L.P.
II. Title.
HQ75.2.P47   1992
306.9'0664—dc20   92-24752
                                                           CIP

10 9 8 7 6 5 4 3 2

Dedicated to

SERGEANT LEONARD MATLOVICH

Congressional Cemetery
Washington, D.C.

The following was presented to
Mr. and Mrs. Leonard C. Matlovich in December 1990:

The United States of America honors the memory of Leonard P.
Matlovich. This certificate is awarded by a grateful nation in recognition of devoted and selfless consecration to the service of our country
in the armed forces of the United States.

George Bush
President
United States of America

Contents

A Brief Introduction to Gay and Lesbian Courage

What is *gay and lesbian* courage? Does it differ from just *ordinary* courage? Perhaps only in application. But that covers a considerable spectrum.

In his book *Profiles in Courage*, John F. Kennedy tended to define courage as it applies to politics. For Kennedy, a courageous politician was one who did what he or she was morally elected to accomplish—"the right thing"—even in the face of danger to the individual's own political career. However, for gay men and for lesbians everywhere, courage must have a wider, considerably more varied application.

An old College Edition of *Webster's New World Dictionary of the American Language* defines courage as "1. the attitude or response of facing and dealing with anything recognized as dangerous, difficult, or painful, instead of withdrawing from it; quality of being fearless or brave; valor; pluck. 2. (*Obs.*), mind; purpose; disposition; spirit; temper; the courage of one's convictions, the courage to do what one thinks is right."

The New American *Roget's College Thesaurus* lists a considerable number of synonyms for "courage," including these nouns: bravery, valor, resoluteness, spirit, daring, gallantry, heroism, defiance of danger; audacity, nerve, pluck, mettle; fortitude, firmness, stability; perseverance, backbone, and spunk. Among adjectives, synonyms for "courageous" include: stouthearted, iron-hearted, lion-hearted; enterprising, adventurous, venturesome, strong-minded, hardy, determined, dogged, indomitable, gritty, and bold as brass. They are words by which many of our friends should forever be remembered.

In the following chapters, we submit stories of courage with which we are personally acquainted. These individuals have achieved recognition in various fields—because of intentional bravery, by the example of their lives and, sadly, on occasion, because of untimely death. Our heroes and heroines should be considered representative, each in his or her own way, of a vast multitude of similar, unheralded lesbians and gay men whose names most of us will never know, but whose ambition and achievements, whose hopes, sorrows, aspirations, and frustrations are echoed countless times each day among more than twenty-five million gay men and women who reside in the United States of America—and among countless millions more who live all around the world subject to various degress of liberation or subjugation.

Courage is a state of mind most often manifested by those among us who are not necessarily prominent, powerful, or wealthy. Courage is something that guides us only from within ourselves. Our mettle is tested when we are under siege by people who would harm us physically or psychologically, be the assault from politicians, civil servants, common bullies, bigots, or even from those who should know better—parents, friends, lovers, and those who profess to save our souls.

Within the ranks of all religious denominations, including those led by infamous, hate-spouting, professional preachers, be assured that there are *many* thousands of closeted homosexual ministers. We have met them face-to-face, and we have met them in vast numbers, but we are not enriched by the encounters or intimidated by their false claims of virtue. They are not brave or gallant soldiers of divinity. They deceive no one more than they delude their shadowy selves. They abuse their own integrity by not disavowing the ignoble, unloving pronouncements of a few dangerously successful fundamentalist religious leaders with intentionally twisted theology.

We have met the incognito homosexual hypocrites away from their homes, skulking in big cities, indulging themselves in the halls that they, not we, call sinful. Our regard would be greater for such pathetic individuals if they had the fortitude to say, "I am married (or engaged, or single), and I am unhappy because I have cheated or lied or condemned others for what I myself do in private." How much better this world would be if those closeted, double-faced individuals would come out into the open and repent, not of being themselves, but repent of their hypocrisy! A little courage from more gay and lesbian Baptist, Catholic, Mormon, and other Christians (who—don't ever doubt it!—are with us in *large* numbers) would be a good reason for joy.

Think how much suffering that one man—the Pope in Rome—could instantly dissipate by rising above nonintellectual homophobia and simply admitting the plain and obvious truth, that Jesus Christ never once spoke against God's homosexual children. Such a fair and unhedged declaration from any leader of the faith would inscribe that person's name on heaven's roll call.

Rarely is there any greater form of courage, anywhere

or anytime, in any area of personal relationships, including vocational fields of endeavor, than the courage of the child who finally concludes that the moment has arrived when it is essential to explain to a parent (1) that his or her sexuality is contrary to what society holds to be a norm; (2) that he or she can never be part of the nongay majority; and (3) that he or she cannot always be part of a masquerade, strangling in the debilitating pretense of heterosexuality that heterosexual parents inherently expect. On such an occasion raw courage is likely to be required because, often, the parent, almost certainly a displeased recipient of unwelcome information, takes the position that the person revealing his own or her own sexual identity is taking such action in order to hurt and punish—an erroneous conclusion and a far cry from the truth. Such an unfortunate assumption on the part of the parent or guardian is nearly always incorrect because, no matter how severe the hurt may be to the parent, the hurt to the offspring has been and may continue to be considerably worse. Imagine the months, years, sometimes decades of torment the average gay or lesbian child endures before fearfully deciding that her or his only prescription for mental health includes personal honesty (with family acceptance desirable, but not required). Realize that within the son or daughter's goal of independent existence coexists the desperate hope that the recipient of what once was secret knowledge can remain (or become) a helpful, totally loving, partially understanding friend, relative, or guardian.

Were all parents sensitive, knowledgeable, and caring, gay children would not need the courage required to free themselves from a quagmire of sexual intolerance that often begins at home. The problem is, however, that to initiate the process of becoming a parent, there rarely exists any noble justification. An act of procreation, like other fleeting biological urges (no matter how we may try to glorify the process), is and always will be one of the most basic of animal instincts. Sexual union requires neither intelligence nor care, tenderness, or love, and the entire exercise can be—and often is, unfortunately—nothing more than a passionate heterosexual misuse of temporarily inflated, lustfully lubricated, genital equipment. So it is common to have selfish fathers and mothers who have no idea how to parent, who never know or have any realization in their narrowly educated, wildly prejudiced, heterosexual heads that some supreme pelvic commandment did not endow them with much in the way of sexual education (or sexual understanding) to accompany their unremarkable sexual drives. The result is that gay children, in a very real struggle for environmental stability, quickly perceive that upon their declaration of homosexuality, parental rejection and abuse is a very real possibility.

Lesbian and gay children have been forced of necessity into the startling realization that many adults are emotionally unable to handle truth about the birds and bees. The result is that it takes a lot of fortitude to attempt any well-intentioned explanation of homosexuality to sometimes belligerent or resentful adults, including parents, who routinely worship heterosexual institutions and wedding anniversaries, while on the other hand, in the most surprising and unanticipated admissions, reveal, that although they have managed sexual intimacies, they still do not have the slightest notion of what true love is all about.

We have also been rudely brought to the realization that another major source of gay difficulties, resulting in defensive, defiant courage, is often the police, acting individually or in groups. For some reason, interspersed throughout history, there have been institutionally protected bullies who see it as their duty to hurt and punish people who openly admit to homosexual desires or engage in gay lifestyles. The gendarmes' degree of zeal has, naturally, varied according to time and place, yet mistreatment of gay and lesbian people has frequently been prevalent, even when real and important dangers to civilization exist. Police attention, if focused on persistent nongay problems, could greatly benefit society. Attacks upon generally law-abiding gay and lesbian people have never accomplished any public good. Quite the contrary.

It is not easy for lone individuals to stand against unjust laws and resist the callous legions of society enjoying their own methods of enforcement. In the United States we are shamed by instances when unprotected gay people have been the intentional victims of uniformed police officers. Even capital crimes have happened all too often.

We recall with horror how a defenseless fellow in handcuffs outside of Los Angeles' Dover Hotel died one night because a vicious policeman cursed and called him "fruit"—while doing knee-drops on the man's unprotected stomach, splitting the pancreas! The court hearing that followed was a blatant whitewash; there were no video cameras to document the sickening event.

In Texas, a gay man with his hands handcuffed behind his back was thrown by "fairy"-hating police into a raging river. To nobody's surprise, the gay man drowned. "Trying to escape" was the explanation of the officers, cheered on by rabid members of the local Ku Klux Klan. That very familiar line might have been accepted had not relatives of the deceased been sufficiently inflamed to bring *civil* charges. His family won their case against "law enforcement" officers.

Our list of injustices is long and could fill more pages than we desire. However, our objective is not to unduly criticize police officers; we realize that the preponderance of those dedicated men and women deserve medals for their service to the community, not words of condemnation. The same is true of a majority of mothers, fathers, and ministers. The reason for decrying a sad minority of preachers, parents, and police is to stress, by contrast, the dynamic roles of protagonists who oppose them—our courageous gay and lesbian friends who inhabit the pages that follow.

We want our readers to realize how difficult it is to be courageous, and at the same time to become aware of how often that distinction is achieved by our gay sisters and brothers in all walks of life—be they retiring in personal manner or holding hands in public. We want you to be able to look at a flamboyant gay man or lesbian woman in some gaudy, possibly tasteless costume, prancing before a Gay Pride parade float, and not think, "Jesus, save us from that creature!" It would be considerate, and wiser, to understand that his or her bravado represents more courage than you or we may even be able to appreciate. That gay person is on stage for all of us (whether we like it or not) to proclaim to the world that we exist, that we have a right to be different, each in our own way. With every hard-won step toward tolerance and justice comes a little more freedom for all; and that "stereotypical" person out in front is doing something for everybody. That person has a right to exist and is telling the world that we too have a right to exist, each in separate fashion. What's more, that person is catching the backlash, not us. That person is bearing the "slings and arrows of outrageous fortune" to a greater degree than anybody else. It takes a lot of courage. Remember, and be proud. That ostentatious individual is a valuable leader on the road to liberation.

Not too long ago in America the only places we could gather were lesbian and gay bars, and none too safely. Dangerous gangs on the streets assaulted us arriving and departing. Inside, vice officers were playing "games," making arrests when gay people did no more and no less than nongay people did in nongay bars. As a testament to stupidity, there were police raids, with gay people lined up against the walls like criminals, repeatedly searched, cursed, and abused. Yes, this is true. Our only error may be one of understatement. In these cases, the heroes were often bartenders, a strange breed of "defiant queers" who somewhere, perhaps in their profession, were among the first who learned to resist both the civil establishment and those agents of law enforcement who intimidated almost everybody else. It is impossible to forget bartenders who, facing arrest, would stand before intruding uniformed police and, with little regard for their personal safety, vigorously remind gay patrons in the bars of their constitutional rights which were repeatedly being violated with impunity. It is more than probable that those particular bartenders were the real progenitors of gay liberation. They imbued many of us with the mettle to stand up to corrupt authority, and, as we matured, the backbone to separate right from wrong and to demand that public officials also take notice of the difference.

Often as not, acts of courage are performed as part of the function of making a living. Not every gay person has the privilege of becoming a lawyer, doctor, corporate executive, or movie star. Many have to improvise, resulting in a vast array of individual businesses that are gay- or lesbian-owned and operated.

Among the most important vocational endeavors in recent years were publications that concerned themselves with identifiable subgroups. Newspapers and magazines that eventually became popular were not moneymakers in the beginning. There was no network of retail outlets willing to sell them. Consequently, it is reasonable to conclude that the early publishers had the welfare, enlightenment, and entertainment of the gay community at heart—goals that have not necessarily carried over to the present. In the beginning, publishers of newsworthy lesbian and gay periodicals had to constantly contend with and resist being put out of business. They were constantly in danger of losing everything they owned to creditors—and because of what they printed, in danger of arrest (which did occur) and possible imprisonment. The courage of journalists has been of inestimable value to the emergence of a well-informed gay community.

There are many types of courage. There are lesbian mothers who have fought for custody of their children; there are homosexual attorneys who have fought to rescue their gay brothers and sisters from the stigma of illegal and unfair arrest; there are producers who have striven to honestly portray gay characters on television and in motion pictures; there are healthy volunteers who associate and work with terribly ill AIDS patients on a daily basis; there are ordinary male or female couples who face unsympathetic neighbors and proclaim, wordlessly, we are gay, we are lesbian, and we are proud; there are lesbian Christians, gay Jews, and homosexual members of many other faiths who worship in the sight of God and know that however they are persecuted, they are loved by their Creator!

Completing a list of examples of gay and lesbian courage would be an exhausting endeavor. Let us agree that courage comes wrapped in many packages, and that—perhaps because of adversity, perhaps because of centuries of unfair discrimination—the lesbian and gay minority, so creative in ways other than biological, has on the one hand become frightened, on the other, brave. We pray that valor, in the future, will prevail.

With the understanding that one can never do justice to the entire community, we nevertheless pay tribute by presenting stories of a courageous, representative handful of residents. Four are gay men. Four are lesbians. Some are famous and others are not. All are people we are proud to call our own.

Kill a Queer
for Christ

"Kill a Queer for Christ" proclaimed bumper stickers in Miami, Florida, during Anita Bryant's successful political crusade against gay people in the spring of 1977. Nobody will ever know how many receptive and malleable malcontents reacted to that murderous suggestion, but there is little doubt that it was at least symptomatic of a widespread and socially sanctioned immorality that became dramatically focused one and a half years later in California.

On the 27th of November, 1978, Dan White, a handsome, humorless, thirty-two-year-old ex–city supervisor (as well as ex-fireman, ex-policeman) intentionally bypassed metal detectors by climbing through a window in San Francisco's City Hall. Dan White carried a concealed .38 caliber Smith & Wesson revolver plus extra bullets in his pocket. Once inside the public building, White gained unaccompanied admission into a private, inner office where, without warning, he fired four times at defenseless Mayor George Moscone, rapidly reducing the latter to a blood-drenched corpse. Then White reloaded his revolver and hurried down the hallway in search of his second victim, Harvey Milk, San Francisco's first openly gay city supervisor.

The motive for White's first murder was mostly a matter of revenge. He had resigned from San Francisco's Board of Supervisors, and the resignation had been accepted by Mayor Moscone. Later, when White changed his mind and decided he wanted to resume the office to which he had been elected, Moscone refused to reinstate the unhappy, unstable ex-supervisor.

White's animosity toward Harvey Milk, however, was more complicated. The unseated supervisor's anger existed not only because Harvey had urged the mayor to side against White, but also because of the celebrated fact that Harvey was open about his homosexuality and proud to be gay, a situation White and his "choirboy" friends might have grudgingly tolerated had they not felt threatened by the irritating fact that Milk was exceptionally good at his job—a bona fide success, well-liked by constituents, gay and otherwise. Harvey was politically adept, and obviously becoming more powerful than many established nongay individuals in San Francisco. As a result, cliques, including antigay firemen, stolid businessmen, and real-estate speculators (in addition to the ubiquitous police), had frequently directed verbal, homicidal poison into Dan White's receptive ears, and were the guilty, unnamed accessories to his infamous double homicide.

The final scene of carnage was ugly in the extreme. To protect himself, Milk had raised his arms in front of his body. It was a futile attempt. One of the first hollow-tip bullets fired by White penetrated Harvey's right wrist and cut through his midsection. Two more dum-dums slammed into the gay politician's chest. He fell, screaming. A bullet went through the back of his head, splattering the room with blood. Then White put the muzzle of his Police Special against Harvey's skull and blew out the remainder of the "faggot's" brains!

Soon everyone would know what had transpired; but in the meantime, the assassin, taking advantage of ensuing confusion, fled.

Twenty-five tumultuous minutes had elapsed when Dianne Feinstein, distraught and shaken, spoke to reporters. "As president of the Board of Supervisors," she said amid the crush of media personnel, "it is my duty to make this announcement: Both Mayor Moscone and Supervisor Harvey Milk have been shot and killed."

In another five minutes, at a police station where he anticipated that his reception would be friendly, Dan White, embraced by his concerned wife, turned himself in. As expected, he was hurried into protective custody. (It has been recorded, reliably, that approving officers patted the killer on his buttocks like a conquering football hero.) The homophobic ex-cop had returned to his own.

Day faded into the chill of evening. Silent mourners began to assemble at the corner where Castro Street crosses Market, the place known today as Harvey Milk Plaza. People who came were of all ages, a cross section of Americans with differing sexual realities, all joined together in sadness. With them they brought candles, which they lighted; and when their numbers swelled into the tens of thousands, they began to tread solemnly through the quiet streets where business had ceased and the doors were locked. As far as the eye could see, for miles, people were pouring into the thoroughfare, a flood of humanity which advanced relentlessly toward the center of the city.

Leading the procession, wearing a black arm band, was

one solitary drummer beating a steady, mournful dirge. And from a balcony came the eerie sound of a muted trumpet that played "Blowin' in the Wind." It was accentuated by a tangible melancholy in the night.

Police were ready for trouble, but they misread the mood of the crowd. Trouble would come later. On that November evening, hours after the assassination, there was only grief, sadness, shock—the feeling of loss and despair tempered with a glimmer of hope that Harvey Milk's death might not have been in vain.

Forty thousand people peaceably assembled at City Hall in tribute to the gay martyr. As a participant observed, on that clear night with thousands of candles held by the multitude, it looked as though half the stars in heaven had become flickering tributes in the streets of San Francisco.

Dianne Feinstein spoke to the huge gathering. "Harvey was a leader who represented your voices," said the woman who would be Mayor. "Remember him for his commitment, for his humor, and for his ability to develop a sense of destiny. I ask you to take up that legacy."

A statement from Jimmy Carter was read. The President of the United States referred to Harvey Milk as a "hardworking and dedicated Supervisor, a leader of San Francisco's gay community who kept his promise to represent all constituents." President Carter also verbalized his "outrage and sadness at the senseless killing" of both politicians.

There was no unseemly demonstration.

Joan Baez sang "Swing Low, Sweet Chariot" with penetrating beauty, bringing tears to grief-stricken eyes. When the tribute at City Hall ended, the crowd dispersed. Left behind at the base of the statue of a weary, resolute Abraham Lincoln were hundreds of small wax candles creating a temporary glow.

*   *   *

In the weeks that followed, sorrow evolved into a pervasive, silent rage. A resident effectively described the situation when he said that "a sense of doom developed." Unquestionably, there came to be a gut feeling that legality, and not justice, would prevail.

Apprehension increased in the gay community when some policemen began openly flaunting T-shirts imprinted with the words "Free Dan White." There were also other indications that the rule of law, as had happened so often in the past, would fail to punish someone who violently harmed a known homosexual.

San Francisco's "peace" officers were instrumental in raising $100,000 for a Dan White Defense Fund. Off-duty policemen were amused to chant, "Dan White—is all right!—Dan White—is all right!" And worse, but much to the point, old-fashioned, sometimes brutal, harassment of gay men and lesbians was renewed as normal police activity.

When a gay activist brought legal action protesting mistreatment by officers in uniform, he was snidely asked by a desk sergeant on duty, "How long do you expect to live?" Everywhere in the Bay City the calendar was being turned back to the years when disenfranchised minorities had no civil rights.

In the trial of Dan White, singularly held for two separate murders, each in the first degree, it was not surprising that what transpired was a low mark in the history of jurisprudence. San Francisco's ever-growing gay community and many members of the press believed that justice was never intended to be done. The prosecuting District Attorney continually seemed to mishandle the case. Composition of the jury was allowed to consist almost entirely of persons who might be inclined to favor the defendant.

Any person with a political point of view different from that of Dan White and his peers was summarily dismissed, and gays and other minorities were excluded from the panel of jurors.

The defendant's tape-recorded confession, played in court by the prosecution, sounded more like defense than condemnation, working only to the advantage of Dan White's lawyers. The calculating assassin's self-told tale was so cleverly contrived that upon hearing it, four of the jurors openly wept for the killer.

Another frustrating incident occurred when one of the five psychiatrists hired by the defense off-handedly testified that Dan White was such a "fine gentleman" that he would not stoop to punching his victims in the nose. The argument seemed to be that in order to avoid impolite physical contact, White used a pistol instead! In defending his actions, White himself declared, "Harvey kind of smirked at me and I just got all flushed and hot—and I shot him."

White was portrayed as a family man, a devout ex-policeman whose main crime was unbalancing his body's sugar levels by eating too many sweets, particularly Twinkies, and drinking too much Coca-Cola. This is remembered as the infamous "Twinkie Defense." It would have been unacceptable to almost any jury except one predisposed to favor the defendant. Apparently most of the jurors allowed themselves to believe Dan White was the All-American Boy—with a sugar problem!

Throughout the trial, the jury continued to absorb every silly statement propounded in defense of the politely smiling, clear-eyed defendant who (incidentally) happened to be an unrepentant killer. After little deliberation, the jury found White guilty, not of murder in the first degree, but of manslaughter, a relatively minor crime. Their verdict clearly proclaimed that where San Francisco's court was concerned, White's victims—only a homosexual and his political associate—were of little value. Thus, for the bloody, premeditated crime, Dan White would be locked up for only five years, a penalty not unlike that for an automobile driver convicted of felony "hit and run."

When their infuriating mockery of justice was announced, it was enthusiastically applauded by White's homophobic friends. Onlookers could only wonder: Is it not so bad to kill if, when you commit murder, included among the slain is a victim who admittedly made love to another being of the same gender? Is criminal intent reduced if you "Kill a queer for Christ"?

In all the history of the world, there had only been one gay riot. That violent disorder occurred in June 1969 on Christopher Street in New York's Greenwich Village when gay men and lesbians rebelled against heavy-handed, extortion-minded police who degraded their lives. In San Francisco, a full decade later, intense anger erupted upon disclosure of the assassin's negligible jail sentence, and Harvey's friends braced themselves for America's second rebellious explosion from an angry gay community.

Emerging from an office where he had temporarily gone into seclusion after being stunned by the slap-on-the-wrist verdict from Dan White's jury, Harry Britt, the gay city supervisor appointed to fill Milk's vacant position, made a public statement. "Harvey Milk knew he would probably be assassinated," said Britt. "Harvey knew that the lowest nature in human beings would rise up and get him—but he never imagined this city would approve of that act! It is beyond immoral—it is obscene!"

Almost simultaneously, infuriated protesters began gathering in the Castro, hub of Harvey's constituency. "Out of the bars!" men and women began shouting. "Into the streets!" Soon a person with a bullhorn arrived. "Manslaughter is all they gave Dan White!" he proclaimed. "The bastard got away with murder! Do you think that's all right?"

"No! No! It's not all right!" was the shouted reply.

Relentlessly, a crowd grew. It began like an infant hurricane, churning through the neighborhood, past bars and shops where patrons came out and joined the burgeoning force. A few police saw what was happening but, as usual, misread the early warnings. They were not afraid—they had seen gay parades before. They figured the "fruits" would stomp around, light candles, sing songs, and go home when they were tired.

Soon a thousand gays, some with protest signs, were moving through the streets, jamming several blocks, chanting, gaining momentum, and fueling their anger. Streetlights were turned on as daylight faded. Chants rose and fell. "Avenge Harvey Milk!" the growing mob began to shout, raising its fists. Five thousand furious people started marching out of their ghetto, leaving the Castro, heading once again for City Hall, the scene of so many previously peaceful, futile protests.

At last San Francisco's authorities became alarmed. Police officers were called to consult with city officials somewhere inside the imposing government structure that was soon the center of attack. Rocks began to pelt the building, breaking windows on the first floor. Nonviolent gays were caught between baton-wielding lawmen on one side, and on the other, demonstrative forces unleashed from the gay community. Outnumbered gay leaders clasped arms and formed a human chain with their own bodies, struggling to separate the gay mob from City Hall's front entrance. Miraculously, they held their line until a flying wedge of riot police reached them. But then, in an unanticipated act of ignorance, the officers began clubbing and hauling away the moderate gay leaders. With them went the only hope of avoiding a full-scale riot—and hell broke loose!

"Kill Dan White! Kill Dan White!" screamed the surging mob, totally out of control. A gilded metal grill was jimmied and pried from the door of City Hall. Fire was started beneath a tree. Bottles and other missiles filled the air. People shouted, and screamed, and were injured.

Gay men in helmets broke windows on a line of police cars and methodically arsoned one vehicle after another. Twelve squad cars in a line were eventually burning, their sirens emitting piercing wails until the devices melted. One after another, gas tanks on the vehicles exploded. It was war!

With reinforcements, the police advanced in waves, thrusting themselves into the crowd, beating anyone within reach. Skirmishes were fought everywhere. Gays wrenched chrome bumpers from vehicles and used them for battering rams. Asphalt torn from the streets became missiles. Tree branches served as clubs. The tops of garbage cans were shields. And the battle raged.

Supervisor Britt, during the hours of tumult, faced television cameras and spoke to the people of San Francisco. "The violence that started all this was Dan White's violence," he said. "I feel the jury was violent this afternoon by treating Dan White the way nobody is ever going to believe they would have treated a black person, or a Jewish person, or somebody who did not fit Dan White's image. They were saying that the spirit of Dan White—with all its meanness—is okay. And in so doing, they were very violently attacking the memory of George Moscone and Harvey Milk. We are reacting with anger!"

Many anguished gay men and women, feeling betrayed by a system of justice which had failed to support them, were in total sympathy with the rioters. Every individual gay person venting his or her wrath in San Francisco was multiplied by a thousand more lesbians or gays within the United States who joined in spirit with the protesters.

Nongays expressed outrage because property was damaged, but as one of Milk's friends said on Public Television, "You can replace a door, shrubbery, and police cars. But we can't replace Harvey!"

As the night wore on, people in the streets learned that you cannot long resist real weapons with those you improvise. When clouds of tear gas rolled through the night, and while combatants were silhouetted against flame and smoke, arrests were made. Inevitably, the armed gendarmerie regained control.

More than fifty police were hospitalized. Gays suffered twice as many injuries. That night the police pretended they had won a victory, but they had not. On the following evening, thousands of gay men and women returned to the Castro's streets, this time to celebrate what was coincidentally the birthday of Harvey Milk. Gung-ho members of the police wanted to needlessly disrupt the peaceful celebration, but were commanded to keep their distance.

San Francisco's riot of May 21, 1979, foretold the beginning of the end for the city's antiquated order of selective law enforcement. The stereotypical picture of homosexuals as "pansies" would never be quite the same again. Soon the police department, which had often harmed, harassed, and belittled gay people, was forced to require that one of every seven of its new law enforcement recruits be either gay or lesbian.

Upon release from prison, White, the coddled assassin, discovered that he was generally unwelcome in society, and succeeded in taking the life of a third person—his own. It was an act of desperation. All the world's redneck police could not free White from the rottenness within. Shunned even by fair-weather friends, Dan White's only accomplishment was making a martyr of his gay political enemy.

Supervisor Harvey Milk was not famous until he was murdered. There had been indications he would have liked to be Mayor of San Francisco, and he also enjoyed the idea of holding a Congressional office in Washington, D.C. Maybe all of that would have been possible. Harvey had powerful support among some politicians who were not averse to working with a man capable of delivering a large block of primarily gay votes. Only with his death could everybody see the shattered potential of the gay Jew from New York City.

Harvey was not handsome, but he had the look of someone who cared about people. There was sincerity in his eyes, magnetism in his handshake. And of himself, Harvey gave everything. He ran for public office four times and was only elected once—in the final, overwhelmingly successful attempt. His clothes were often purchased secondhand, and he enjoyed few luxuries, yet, when elected, his own generosity was evident. To ardent supporters he stated triumphantly, "This is not my victory—it is yours. If a gay man can win, it proves there is hope for all minorities who are willing to fight!"

The public's awareness of Harvey Milk was limited to San Francisco until a gubernatorial aspirant named John Briggs, with Anita Bryant for his inspiration, mounted an attack on gay teachers in California. Briggs initiated a statewide vote (Proposition 6) to require that gays, lesbians, and their casual defenders and outspoken sympathizers be fired if they held teaching positions or school-related employment.

For gay people, even those accustomed to cyclical attacks from ambitious bigots, the times were dangerous. "Look what happened to gays in Hitler's Germany," commented Harvey. "Anita Bryant already says that Jews and Moslems are going to hell. You know she's got a shopping list!" It was, therefore, as much in fear as in anger that City Supervisor Milk debated State Senator John V. Briggs on television.

The Senator was no match for Harvey. When Briggs trotted out his last-ditch cliché (arguing that law-abiding homosexuals are evil because they are role models for children), Harvey replied, "I was born of heterosexual parents. I was taught by heterosexual teachers. Then why am I homosexual? If I am the product of role models, I should have been a heterosexual to your way of thinking!"

After the votes were finally counted, Senator Briggs' Proposition 6 was defeated 59 percent to 41 percent. It was a major victory—California's proof that a clear-thinking electorate can assert itself in a free society.

"To the gay community all over this state," said Harvey at a tumultuously happy rally on election evening, "remember that a lot of nongay people joined us to reject Briggs' Initiative. Now we owe them something. We must destroy the myths about homosexuals. Let us shatter the myths once and for all!

"Most importantly, every gay person must come out! As difficult as it is, you must tell your immediate family. You must tell your relatives. You must tell your friends if, indeed, they are your friends. You must tell your neighbors. You must tell the people in the stores you shop in. Then, once they realize we really are their children, and that we are everywhere, every myth, every lie, every innuendo will be destroyed.

"And you will feel so much better."

In the Castro neighborhood where Harvey was elected to San Francisco's Board of Supervisors, his grass-roots constituents were primarily gay men. They cared not that Harvey was graduated from a New York teachers college in 1951 or had been a Lieutenant (j.g.) in the United States Navy. They probably had no knowledge that Harvey had once been a highly regarded financial analyst for Bache & Co. on Wall Street. What they did know was more to the point.

In the last decade of his existence, Harvey had chosen to live in the middle of a gay Mecca. He fiercely wanted to be a politician, and he wanted to use the inherent power of office to represent the electorate. He was a brilliant speaker with a sense of humor. He loved theater, lived drama, attended opera, and enjoyed a sense of tragedy. Although late in coming out of the closet, Harvey never thereafter denied the demands of his sexuality. He was rarely without a lover. When one boyfriend moved on, another moved in.

Toward the end of 1972, Harvey rented a Victorian storefront. The building provided him with space for a little business named Castro Camera, a home (upstairs), and, eventually, headquarters for his grossly underfunded political campaigns.

Vociferously homosexual in his bids for political office, Harvey managed to alienate most of the city's conservative gay leaders, who, he contended, had complacently ignored members of their own community while supporting nongays with a liberal veneer. "You are never given power," Harvey often admonished. "You must take it!" He wrote, "It is time the gay community stops playing with itself and gets down to the real thing. There are people who are satisfied with crumbs because that is all they think they can get. In reality, if they demand the real thing, they will find they indeed can have it."

Harvey continually urged support for lesbian and gay candidates in general, and himself in particular. His distrust for outsiders who could turn against gay people when it was politically expedient was the cornerstone of everything he believed.

On the other hand, established gay power brokers, sedate, sometimes rich, and operating on a slower timetable (with many outstanding gay victories to their credit—such as passage of California's outstanding Consenting Adults Bill) felt Milk might undo much of what had been laboriously accomplished. Consequently, they were rarely even warm toward his political ambitions. Nevertheless, on Harvey's first try for office, he received seventeen thousand votes, which were about sixteen thousand more votes than the most optimistic election analysts had predicted.

In California's big city by the Golden Gate, all kinds of people suddenly realized there actually existed large numbers of lesbians and gay men who would actually go to polling places and vote in support of their own gay candidate! The revelation shocked many and frightened others.

"It takes no survey to remove repression," explained Harvey during one of his discourses, "but it does take an electorate—which is another word for power." To gain more votes in his second campaign, Harvey, who for several years had adopted the look of an aging hippie, again began to cut his hair and "renormalize" his mode of dress. "Appearance, and lots of publicity, are part of the game," he told any leftover flower children who cared to listen.

Simultaneously, from all over America gays were coming to San Francisco, arriving in great numbers. Harvey and his friends worked continuously, getting thousands of newcomers registered to vote. And, when the local Teamsters boycotted Coors in a tough contract dispute, Harvey initiated a signal to gay beer drinkers throughout the American West, persuading the community to support truck drivers by refusing to sell or purchase Coors beer. The boycott was a great success. Thereafter, gay people continued to work with the Teamsters and received a fair share of Teamster jobs, plus votes on election day from members of the union.

When disgruntled residents moved out of the Castro to distance themselves from the "new element," homosexuals happily filled the vacuum, and property values soared. Once again, real estate was the new California gold rush. Everybody was making money—everybody except Harvey. Harvey was earning votes.

By the end of 1975, nearly 150,000 out-of-the-closet gay men and lesbians were living in San Francisco, comprising 20 percent of the city's permanent population; and if Harvey Milk didn't shake the hand of every man and woman in the street, or meet them in his camera store, the adept, would-be politician was sufficiently media-wise to make certain that all residents of the Castro either saw him speaking on their behalf on television or read about him in various newspapers.

It was during that period when an honorably discharged G.I. named Oliver William Sipple, once the lover of a close friend of Harvey, was unexpectedly propelled into national prominence. On September 22, 1975, Billy Sipple, who generally disliked crowds, had been standing near the front of a group waiting outside the St. Francis Hotel to see the President of the United States. As Chief Executive Gerald Ford emerged and moved toward a limousine, Sipple was shocked to glimpse a woman raise a loaded pistol and point it at the President. The range was so close that it was unlikely she would miss her target. Without any consideration for his own safety, Billy Sipple immediately thrust himself in front of the weapon and struggled with the woman, causing the bullet she fired to go harmlessly astray. Alerted to danger only after the struggle began, the U.S. Secret Service quickly shoved President Ford into a waiting limousine and hustled him away.

Days passed, and while national attention was focused on the incident, there was every reason to believe President Ford would have the graciousness to thank the young man who saved his life, perhaps even invite Billy to the White House. Unfortunately, once newspapers discovered Sipple was gay, and then proclaimed in blazing headlines that he was a HOMOSEXUAL HERO, courtesy for Sipple (including any Presidential expression of appreciation) evaporated. A "no comment" was uttered by Gerald Ford, the man President Lyndon Johnson had once described as having "played football too long without a helmet."

The insult to Sipple was also an insult to all gay and lesbian people, and it was too blatant for Harvey Milk to ignore. Never one to shrink from having his say, he fired off an angry telegram addressed to President Ford. The message was not a publicity stunt, and had little appreciable effect—although Billy Sipple did eventually receive a belated, terse note of thanks begrudgingly written by an employee on the President's staff.

A similar homophobic attitude was pervasive at the beginning of the administration of the next President of the United States. When Jimmy Carter came to San Francisco, there was general knowledge among political insiders that he did not want to be photographed with representatives of the gay and lesbian community. So Harvey Milk, not one to be elbowed aside, took his own photographer with him when he went to meet the President—and Harvey obtained a picture of himself shaking hands with Carter. Local antigay politicians scowled from the background, but Jimmy smiled at Harvey! With a camera in his face, the President had few options.

The main issues in government for Harvey were not limited to gay rights, yet gay concerns were always prominently featured on his agenda. "In the future," declared Milk, "no longer should we allow any candidate, even our 'friends,' to evade the gay rights issue merely because supporting gay rights will hurt them with some of the voters!"

Consistent with his belief that power would only be obtained if it was taken, Milk said, "We have fought for the crumbs. Now the establishment has to deal with me. We're overcoming a lot of problems." But privately, a distressing thought plagued the increasingly visible city supervisor—that he might be a target for any number of mentally ill persons. On audiotape he recorded some of his thoughts. Listening to this tape now, we cannot help but feel a chill along the spine as we hear a dead man utter words of precise, prophetic insight.

"If a bullet should enter my brain, let that bullet destroy every closet door!" Harvey said into a tape recorder. The statement, and its fulfillment, illustrate how tremendous was the courage of the politician shouldering his burden of responsibility.

Harvey Milk refused to be diminished by secrecy, nor would he make compromises for his own personal safety. The result was that his constantly increasing political visibility brought a never-ending supply of antigay hate mail (including ugly threats). One letter proclaimed, "Harvey Milk, you will have a nightmare journey to hell. You will be stabbed and have your genitals cut off."

The problem was to decide which warnings were valid and which were not. Harvey soon realized, however, that no one could tell the difference. By the time Harvey ran for office on the fourth, final occasion, he had received so many death threats from "homo-haters" that he accepted the possibility of discovering someday, somewhere, that one of the usually anonymous letter-writers might endeavor to convert threatening words into awful reality.

When Harvey, who liked to call himself the "Mayor of Castro Street," campaigned in 1977, he had little doubt that at last he would be successful. For the first time in recent history, San Francisco had been carved into districts, and its 5th District, which included the well-populated, predominately gay Castro area, was ripe for picking. It had been courted long and successfully by this gay man with a sense of humor who cared not only for those people with whom he was most closely identified but for other ethnic minorities and senior citizens as well. "Harvey made you feel like someone of worth," one schoolteacher recalled.

On election night, forty-seven-year-old Harvey Milk arrived at his victory celebration on the back of a motorcycle that Anne Kronenberg, his young campaign manager, was driving. There was elation everywhere in the Castro that evening. Lesbians and gay men had never felt better—and Harvey, who never drank, playfully sipped from a small glass of champagne and, grinning into the lenses of television cameras, toasted those who were or would become his friends.

"Thank you, San Francisco," Harvey said, sincerely, eloquently, with a very happy smile.

*   *   *

"Will you be a supervisor for all the people?" a reporter asked, even before Milk had settled into his office.

"I have to," replied Harvey. "That's what I was elected for. I have to be here to open up a dialogue for the sensitivities of all people. The problems that affect this city, affect everyone."

Yet of all issues, the one of primary importance to Harvey could only be the Gay Rights Ordinance he wanted for San Francisco. "Its main focus," he said, "is people who are already employed. If they want to come out and break down the stereotypes, the ordinance prevents them from being fired as a result of their candor. For example, you will see our Gay Day parade with at least thirty gay doctors. They are the tip of the iceberg. In the Bay Area there are hundreds and hundreds of gay doctors, mostly closeted because of their fear of losing jobs. In San Francisco, they will be able to come out!"

Harvey predicted his Gay Rights Ordinance would pass easily. It did. Ten of the city's eleven supervisors voted it into law. The only dissenting vote was the Board's Supervisor from District 8, Dan White, who had pouted throughout the proceedings. Following a lopsided vote favoring the gay community, White engaged in a public tantrum and angriliy departed. Soon thereafter, the 1978 Gay Day celebration was held in San Francisco. It was magnificent. As many as four hundred thousand gay men and lesbians were on the sidewalks and in the parade, proud and happy to be free—singing, carrying banners of joy, and generally engulfed in an outpouring of good humor. Milk rode without protection in an open car. "Come on out," he said gently, meaningfully, as a television camera moved into a closeup of the persuasive smile on his face, resembling nothing so much as a Jewish leprechaun.

Considerably more somber, Anne Kronenberg anticipated that something terrible was going to happen. She
was unable to ignore hate mail that continued to pour
into their campaign office. Nor was Anne shy about con-
fiding her fears to Harvey.

"Don't talk about unpleasant things like being shot," he
would reply. "It could happen at any time. I'm just not
going to worry about it." But Harvey did worry in soli-
tude, not only for his own sake but because of what his
position on the Board of Supervisors meant to all the
people in San Francisco who had cast their ballots for
him. Therefore, shortly after being elected, Harvey made
a will—recorded on an audiocassette so that it might be
played for many to hear. The will was an attempt, which
proved not to be in vain, to outline his supervisorial
wishes and to name political heirs, should his followers
need guidance.

"This is Harvey Milk speaking on Friday, November
18, 1977," he said. "I fully realize that a person who
stands for what I stand for, a gay activist, becomes the
potential target for somebody who is insecure, terrified,
afraid, or very disturbed. Knowing I could be assassinated at any time, I feel it's important that some people
know my thoughts.

"I have always considered myself part of a movement.
I've considered the movement to be the candidate. I
think there's a delineation between those who use the
movement and those who are part of the movement. I
would hope the Mayor will understand that distinction—and understand that appointing somebody who
subtly opposed me, or kept quiet, or stuck their head in
the sand, would be an insult to everything I stood for.

"Another aspect is what would happen should there be
an assassination. I cannot prevent people from feeling

angry and frustrated, but I hope they will, instead of demonstrating, take the power. I would like to see every gay lawyer, every gay architect come out, stand up and let the world know. That would do more to end prejudice overnight than anybody could imagine. I urge them to do that. I urge them to come out. Only in that way will we start to achieve our rights.

"I hope there are no religious services. I would turn over in my grave. And it's not a disbelief in God. It's a disbelief and disgust for what most churches are about. How many leaders got up in their pulpits or went to Miami and said, 'Anita Bryant, you're playing gymnastics with the Bible—you're desecrating the Bible'? How many of them said it? How many of them hid and walked away? Ducked their heads in the name of Christianity and talked about Love and Brotherhood?

"If anything, play the tape of Briggs and me over and over so people can know what an evil man is. So people will know what Hitler was like. So people will know where ideas of hate come from. So they'll know what the future will bring if they are not careful!"

The verbal document ended on a note of hope, which Harvey was always careful to include in his addresses. His hope never failed; and even when he feared death, Harvey hoped for life. Yet if he had lived decades longer, his life might not have exceeded the impact of his death. None of us will ever know. What we do understand is that Harvey fought a battle in which he clearly knew of the dangers to himself, and he never shrank from what his integrity demanded. The survival of gay equality depends upon women and men who bring similar wit and compassion into the leadership arena.

Perhaps the brightest aspect of Harvey's personality was his enduring sense of humanity, forever turbulent, caring, sensitive. He was an individual who would never forgo the American Constitution or the Bill of Rights as they are idealistically explained in secondary schools, holding forth the indelible promise of life, liberty, and the pursuit of happiness, with justice for all.

Speaking to those whose convictions may have been less strong, Harvey often said, "In Des Moines or San Antonio—or some other place—there is a young person who all of a sudden realizes he or she is gay, who knows that if the parents find out, he or she will be tossed out of the house, and classmates will taunt the child. The Anita Bryants and John Briggs on TV are also doing harm. So the child has several options: remain in the closet—suicide—come to California—or stay in San Antonio and fight!

"Two days after I was elected, I got a phone call. The voice was quite young. It was from Altoona, Pennsylvania. The person said, 'Thanks—you've made me believe in the Constitution of the United States for the first time ever.'

"So you see, you've got to keep electing gay people for that young child, and the millions upon millions like that child, to know there is hope for a better tomorrow. Not only for gays, but for blacks, Asians, the disabled, our senior citizens, and us!

"Without hope, we give up. I know you cannot live on hope alone, but without it, life is not worth living. You, and you, and you have got to see that the promise does not fade.

"I thank you very much."

We, the People!

"When I was a little kid," recalls Elaine Noble, "I used to take books out of the library and read about New England, the ocean, Massachusetts, Paul Revere, Bunker Hill, the Old North Church, everything. I loved what I read, and I wanted to go and live in Boston."

Years of triumph and moments tinged with terror would pass before a particular day arrived when Elaine was walking toward the State House. It was a beautiful morning with a clear blue sky. An old man with a wooden cane approached from the grassy green of Boston Common. His gnarled fingers reached out. "Are you Elaine Noble?" the grizzled character asked, touching her shoulder.

Like any well-trained politician, Elaine stopped, turned, and stuck out her hand. She was radiant, and unprepared. "I thought one of our senior citizens wanted to shake my hand," Elaine said later, "but the codger scowled, muttered something about me being a lesbian, and spit in my face!"

Ugh!

Public life has always been fraught with the unexpected. Elaine Noble has had more than her share of exciting experiences, and alternately shudders and smiles as she remembers.

"Boston is like a half-baked potato for a diner with a hearty appetite," she lovingly observes. "It may be too hot, but you can't put it down. There are unique things in Boston, too, things that are really wonderful. People here might be the first to knock you down—but then they are also the first to pick you up again.

"There's a whimsy about the Irish. We love to fight. When I was newly elected and untested in public office, it was time for the annual St. Patrick's Day celebration. Every politician has to march in South Boston's parade or lose a wagon-load of votes, and probably lose the next election as well!"

"But, Elaine, you can't march in South Boston!" a senior state senator cautioned.

"Don't do this, Elaine," warned another colleague. "Don't be stupid! The Irish Catholics will kill you! You're for busing—and you're gay! It'll be like running a gauntlet!"

"My God, they'll stone you to death!" declared a close friend.

Elaine considered the unpleasant possibilities and shrugged. "I have to do it," she concluded, resigned to danger. After a few sleepless nights, Elaine received encouraging news. Women employed on the police force had volunteered to work extra duty. Their presence along the parade route would mean that Elaine's courage would now and again be bolstered by a friendly female face saying, "It's okay, sister, things are clear to move along. It's going to be alright."

One policewoman, whose father had been a policeman before her, said to Elaine, "We figured, if you have the guts to try, the least we can do is provide some backup."

Touched by the consideration, Elaine was willing to accept any available protection. "I wasn't stupid enough to want to march by myself," she admitted, "nor was it by accident that I arranged my position to be fairly close behind the Immaculate Conception Band. I hoped that if there was trouble, band members might come to my rescue, or at the least, scream bloody murder!"

Problems were predictable, particularly at one location where the parade turned at a corner. There, on a grassy knoll, gangs of shirtless, semitough, adolescent boys usually sat drinking beer. On this particular St. Patrick's Day, they made their intentions clear. They were waiting for the "gay broad" to try to pass!

As fate would have it, the line of march came to a stop with Elaine close to the knoll. For one of the few times during the morning, no police, not even the women were in sight. Members of the Immaculate Conception Band were otherwise distracted. Only Elaine seemed acutely aware of shouts from unruly, unshaven youths on the grassy knoll.

"Hey, dyke!" some of the rowdy rabble called, waving at Elaine in a mocking fashion, rapidly beginning to formulate what threatened to escalate into dangerous behavior. Elaine knew she was in trouble unless she acted immediately, and being on her own, instinctively realized that an aggressive offense on her part would probably be the best defense. Therefore, without hesitating, she walked briskly to the crowded street corner and pointed up through the snickering adolescents to one of the biggest, brawniest beer drinkers.

"Hey, you!" snapped Elaine, her voice intentionally tough.

"Me?" asked the surprised leader.

"Yeah. You! Come here!"

"Sure—why not?" snickered the cocky young man. With a beer bottle in hand, he did his "strut" down the hill to Elaine. She was taller, and leaned down until their eyes were level and her nose was about six inches away from his. Then, in the sweetest voice anybody has ever heard, Elaine said softly to the suspicious Irish lad, "Can I have a belt of ya beer?"

The surprised drinker stared into Elaine's eyes. When she smiled at him, half the battle was won. The rest of her victory came when she took the bottle he handed to her, tilted its bottom toward the sun, and began chug-a-lugging!

"Dear Lord," thought Elaine, "help me get all of this beer down. Please, help me, God!" Fortunately, the bottle was only two-thirds full. Otherwise, Elaine was certain she would have gagged and failed. The crowd never knew the difference.

"Yeeeaaaahhhh!!!" they screamed—an approving audience. "She did it! She's okay—pass the word—she's okay!"

"Thanks," said Elaine, wiping her mouth and returning the empty bottle. It was her secret that she came so close to being ill.

Elaine Noble was the first openly gay person in America to be elected to any political office on the state level. Her journey from Natrona, Pennsylvania, a grimy, poverty-stricken, company-owned mining town where she was born, to the Boston of her dreams was a memorable trip, not in time or distance but measured in accomplishment.

Thirty miles north of Pittsburgh, Natrona had a river running on one side and ore-rich hills on the other. Below the mines was a railroad track, and for as many miles as the eye could see, there were monotonous rows of small, dingy houses. Ten rows made a village, and each village looked much like its neighbor. The best way to distinguish Natrona from contiguous housing communities was by observing its boundary signs: ENTERING NATRONA was posted at one end and LEAVING NATRONA at the other.

"The huge steel mill dwarfed our entire village. That gave people an idea of how insignificant we were," recalled Elaine. "I always had a sense of being in captivity. There was a feeling that nothing was beyond the river, nothing beyond the hills. And if, by chance, there was something, it would be simply more of the same.

"The majority of workers were immigrants who came directly from the Old World to work in the mines and the mill. They rented a company house, bought from the company store, and went to the company doctor when they were ill. Often, there was no money left over when company bills had been paid."

Unlike their neighbors, Elaine's ancestors came to America before the Civil War. Her mother's family had once owned a fleet of merchant ships, but before she was born, both of Elaine's parents had inherited only the results of adversity. Her Scotch-Irish father, a machinist who struggled to keep his family alive during the Great Depression of the 1930s, was fortunate to have an eighth-grade education. A very nice, gentle man with a love of reading, he later taught himself to read Russian and French.

"We had enough money to keep clothes on our backs, and food, but there were people around us who didn't," Elaine remembers. "Some of the fathers drank. My dad also enjoyed his spirits, but kept everything under control. He held a full-time job and another that was part-time. He was a grievance man for the union and, in our neighborhood, negotiated a lot of community problems. The bookmobile came down our street because my father made a request.

"I remember other things that made him a hero in my eyes. When the workers had a gambling pool going at the mill, paycheck serial numbers were written upon bits of paper, folded into a hat, and a winner was drawn. After a couple of people had ripped off the jackpot, my father was eventually asked to do the drawing. Everybody knew he was an honest man, a reputation he guarded. My father climbed up on a cart, proceeded to give a short, humorous speech on the evils of gambling, then pulled a folded piece of paper out of the hat. As he silently looked at it, perhaps mentally comparing the number with his own, a funny look came over his face. Then without warning, he suddenly poked the paper into his mouth and swallowed it! Well, all hell broke loose! The workers threatened to do fifty kinds of unnatural things to my father to get it back, but finally had to settle for having him pull another. We can only surmise that, by a trick of fate, the first number he pulled had been his own!

"There were no distinctions between children going to school. We were white, black, Polish, Czechoslovakian, and everything else imaginable. There was no such thing as discrimination. Our next-door neighbors spoke only Polish, but were determined their children would speak English. They knew the only way they could get ahead in the United States was to speak the primary language.

"There was a time when I was temporarily sent away from the valley. My brother and sister went with my mother to stay with our grandparents. I went to live with my aunt. Her environment was completely different from the only one I had previously known. For the first time, I saw that living could be a banquet of color, sunshine, and flowers, art and achievement—wonders of life that surpassed the day-to-day struggle for survival I had always observed. It was an exciting step for me, that glimpse up at a middle-class world. Once I had seen the candy store, I knew I could never spend the remainder of my years in Natrona. I knew life offered other options!

"Recently, I took a friend back to that little village. She was a New Yorker. She said, 'Oh, my God! In New York, when you're poor, you can get on a subway or a bus and go to other places for the price of a token—and see what beauty is. But in a place like Natrona, how could you ever get away?'"

Elaine and her brother were fortunate. Upon reaching high school, they became involved in a busing program that transported black and white children of different nationalities to the high school in a community ten miles away, a middle-class oasis in hills overlooking the valley. Their classmates were the sons and daughters of managers, accountants, and lawyers at the mill.

"If it hadn't been for busing, I wouldn't have had a chance to get the education I did," said Elaine. "It gave me an opportunity to learn skills and better myself, which would not have been possible if I'd stayed in the trap where I was born. That's true for a lot of us!"

To earn money for college, Elaine worked on an assembly line, with the task of quality control in a factory that produced ceramic outer linings for underground telephone wires. It was in this industrial setting that she met her first lesbian.

"Kelly was great," Elaine remembers. "She had a motorcycle and a little convertible. Her hair was short, slicked back, and she was such a dyke! I loved Kelly. We enjoyed doing things together, and she was my best friend for a long time. I was seventeen when she brought me out.

"My family really liked Kelly. She frequently came

home with me for dinner, and was always great fun. The family never made any comments about her, but because I had gotten rid of all my boyfriends, my father and mother were beginning to put two and two together.

"I was in the kitchen on a summer evening, with my back turned toward my mother—thank God!—when she said to me, 'Your father wants to know if you're a lesbian.'

"Softly, I said to myself, 'Oh—dear—heaven!' I began to feel prickly heat all over my body. In my hand I was holding a pot, which I put down on the stove, fearing my fingers would lose their grip. Then, in as casual a voice as I could muster under the circumstances, I said, 'Well then, if he wants to know, why doesn't my father ask me?'

"'Good question,' Mother replied.

"I didn't dare turn around, however, because if she had seen the expression on my face during those moments, she would have known the answer. My brother and I could never learn how to lie to her. Mother was very skilled at determining the truth. She seemed to have some kind of X-ray vision. That's why I was afraid to let her look in my eyes. She would have known I was hiding something."

Clarion University is high in Pennsylvania's mountains, where the evergreen is prolific, bear hunting was a sport, and fraternal organizations were popular. Elaine Noble joined Zeta Tau Alpha.

When the queen of Clarion's Laurel Mountain Court was crowned, Elaine—because of her charm and genuine beauty—was chosen to be a princess in attendance. It was part of the acceptable life at the state-funded college. "Outsiders" were those who did not belong to sororities.

"They included lesbians!" said Elaine, reliving the awe she had felt for them. "And they were wild! They would drink and play cards late at night. It was a scandal when they got their dorm mother drunk—that was pretty outrageous! They frightened me half to death—but I thought they were wonderful!

"The dean of the college decided she was going to engage in a 'lesbian scare' and rid the school of homosexuals. What actually happened is that one person, Karen, was expelled. She became the sacrificial lamb. A notation in her permanent scholastic record was made to indicate that she was 'recruiting others to become lesbians'—an unrealistic, inflammatory concept with the poison to ruin the young woman's life for the next decade!"

Years after the incident, Elaine happened to meet Karen again. They were kidding, when Elaine said, "If you were recruiting, why didn't you recruit me?"

Karen laughed. She answered, "I didn't know you were one of us."

"I didn't know, either," Elaine replied. She had never had a sexual relationship with anyone but Kelly, and that briefly, in Natrona. Nonetheless, Elaine was terrified by the overblown threat of a campus purge. "I hadn't ever done anything in all of my freshman year," she said. "I hadn't been involved with a single person—but the dean had me intimidated, and I secretly decided to leave while the leaving was good! I transferred at the end of the year."

Thirty-two degree-granting institutions are located in and around Boston. Elaine chose to continue her education at Boston University, where she was granted a trustee's scholarship. In addition to studies, Elaine worked a couple of part-time jobs. "It didn't leave a heck of a lot of time for socializing," she said. "I went to class in the mornings, worked the noon shift at the Faculty Club as a waitress, returned to classes, then worked the dinner shift. At midnight I went to Sears and Roebuck, where I labored in the mail-order room until seven in the morning. My first class was at eight o'clock. Between times, I caught sleep if I could!

"My major was in Speech and English with a minor in Theater Education. Theater was housed in the School of Fine and Applied Arts, where people on every floor were seriously studying painting, sculpture, voice, music, et cetera. I had never been exposed to those things before. It was heaven! I still like some wonderful people who were teaching there.

"In 1966 I was graduated with a bachelor's degree in Fine Arts and took a teaching job at Colby, a small junior college in rural New Hampshire. There I learned what 'in the closet' means. It was a sad description of me. I thought homosexuality was a phase I was suffering. I thought homosexuality was an obsession and didn't know why God had done it to me.

"Between my brain and my heart there was conflict for years, because while condemning myself, I was also beginning to have relationships with women and was having a wonderful time. Finally, I just said, 'To heck with all this guilt. The only thing crazy is worrying myself sick.' From then on, I resolved to be open about my lifestyle. Let's face it, I could see women older than myself who had lived together for years—and they lived a damn good life!"

Returning to Boston, Elaine earned a master of science and education degree from Emerson College, a master of education degree from Harvard, and entered the University of Massachusetts for a doctorate. "School has always meant freedom to me," explained Noble, "freedom to better yourself."

In a poor neighborhood of Boston that had much in common with Natrona, Pennsylvania (except that the ugly, big-city buildings were vertical instead of horizontal), teenagers at a settlement house were nearly impossible to control. Most were black and Hispanic. One of their less amusing pastimes was to drop Coke bottles filled with water on the heads of white social workers entering the building. Elaine was in her junior year at Boston University and looking for new part-time employment when the work office said to her, "Do you want this job? Nobody else seems interested!"

"I want it," Elaine snapped immediately. "I really do!" That same afternoon, she dodged a Coke bottle and went to work.

"It felt so familiar to me," she said. "I had emotionally been there before, and in some ways it was a chance to relax. At B.U., unlike myself, most of the kids were wealthy. They had expensive cars. I was happy to have a bicycle. The girls were very cosmopolitan. Many came from New York and wore mink coats their fathers had bought for them. I rotated four serviceable outfits. So it was not unpleasant to be paid for working in an environment that was instantly familiar.

"The agency running the settlement house consisted of myself and twelve 'crazy' Jesuits! Mad, mad, mad, mad, mad Jesuits—and I learned to love them dearly! Some of the men had four or five years in, but even though only one would eventually reach his final vows, they really understood things that professionally trained social workers rarely seemed to comprehend.

"Across the street from our project was a nearly full-size duplication of the Cathedral of Notre Dame. During its days of splendor, cardinals had been ordained there. But time had passed it by.

"The Jesuits organized rough gangs in the neighborhood and gave them constructive things to do. We hustled music stores, obtained instruments, and created an arts program. At the same time, I thrived upon my first taste of politics-in-action. It began when I organized the neighborhood mothers to fight four-legged neighborhood pests—vicious creatures that were biting their children at night—big brutes that had to be fought off with baseball bats—diseased rats that came out of the sewers and the city wading pool when there was too much rain!

"In spite of the unhealthy situation, I discovered that politicians really weren't interested in our medical problems. So I gave speeches, and we had street festivals. I organized what was called Dump Day: a threat from everybody in our neighborhood that we would collect all our garbage and unload it on the steps of City Hall. Local parents readily got involved. They loved it. Mothers and fathers loaded their refuse into trucks the Jesuits had commandeered. Every twenty-four hours, increasingly large piles of debris were unloaded on the steps of various municipal buildings. Day after day, our growing mountains of trash were dumped in front of ever more prestigious city structures located closer and closer to downtown, and every advance was reported on television.

"In short order, somebody with authority said, 'Oh, my God, that Noble woman's really going to bury us!' Then Boston's city hall caved in. In no time at all, health officials came into the neighborhood and did what they were paid to do. For myself, it was a vivid social lesson in democracy! It was proof that pressure works. The only people who were disappointed by the termination of our activity were some neighborhood residents who had saved their smelliest garbage for the State House, which was to have been our final destination.

"It was a lot of work—but we took back a neighborhood! As a result, when other issues arose, we developed new strategies, and frequently won. All of us who were involved developed a heady sense of power. It's nice to remember. That was before receiving my degree from Boston University.

"When I returned from New Hampshire in 1968 and began postgraduate work at Emerson College, I found myself drawn back again to the settlement house. I just couldn't stay away and eagerly resumed my involvement in community politics."

During four years beginning in 1970, Elaine was a teacher at Emerson. She was also the considerate individual who often donated spare time and energy to aid the sprightly old ladies of Boston. She had met them in their neighborhoods and came to love them with a respect that was mutual. At Boston University's Medical Center, Elaine was instrumental in the creation of a section where they could drop in for care. Elaine facilitated Meals on Wheels. And she even hassled city hall until they helped her institute a workshop for the old men.

"Those seniors taught me a great deal about living," sighed Elaine, "and they were fascinating. Between all of them, they had done everything! They had seen everything! And just being with them was a great education."

At Emerson College, Elaine accepted her teaching position, but only after first making certain the school's academic hierarchy understood her sexuality. "I wanted them to know I'm homosexual because I didn't want to be in a classroom and have some jerk unexpectedly jump up and say, 'Surprise, surprise, the teacher's queer!' That's why I laid it all out, hoping the administration would not react against me. The result was that they quietly, matter-of-factly, said, 'Elaine, this doesn't bother us.'

"What a relief, for I remembered my freshman year in college and the lesbian purge at Clarion. That ugly scene! I can still close my eyes and visualize the trauma. I don't ever want to be vulnerable that way again. Nor did I want to hide.

"Emerson's faculty probably were fully aware that I was a lesbian. People you grow up with, people who care, they just somehow sense this about you. One of the saddest things, I think, is to see gay people who work so hard to hide their sexuality! Who are they fooling except themselves?"

Despite her candor, the road to liberation was a slow process for Elaine Noble, but by 1970, there was general public knowledge of who she was. Retreat back into the closet was impossible. Elaine became the advisor of record to a campus homophile group, and she organized Boston's first Gay Pride Parade, in which fewer than thirty-six brave and frightened persons participated. (Today the count exceeds forty thousand.)

With a handful of other dedicated souls, Elaine put together Boston's first homosexual health clinic, which came to be called the Gay and Lesbian Counseling Service, a vigorous organization that never turns anybody away. From Boston University she produced and hosted "Gay Way," a radio program that was popular for years.

During that same period, Elaine and her lesbian friends were informed by the Homophile Union of Boston that they could be a part of that men's organization—but would not be permitted to vote. Definitely unenthusiastic about becoming a "brownie-baking ladies' auxiliary," the women asserted their independence and founded the Boston chapter of Daughters of Bilitis. However, because DOB was primarily interested in socializing and in subtle social change, Elaine and her friends' desire to "belong and be counted" prompted them to turn to a predominately white, middle-class women's organization that did (and still does) play a significant role in the United States—the National Organization for Women.

"Some of us helped to form local chapters of NOW," declared Elaine, "but afterward, NOW gave us a really bad time. As lesbians, we were told to get out—in no uncertain terms. It was dreadful! On the rebound, we went to the first meeting of the Woman's Political Caucus, an organization designed for women who purely want to be political, be they Democrat or Republican. I was accompanied by fifty or sixty other lesbians who wanted to be involved. There were more of us than there were heterosexual women. We filled every workshop. When the time came to vote, I was elected to one of three chairs, causing a group of nongay women to freak out. They couldn't believe we had pulled it off. Frankly, we could hardly believe it either!

"That was my first experience working with heterosexual females. One of them was Ann Lewis, who tops my list of the smartest political people I know. Ann Lewis became, and remains, one of my dearest friends."

Barney Frank was Ann's brother. When Barney ran for state office, Elaine worked on his campaign. In Barney's search for votes, she took him to his first gay political meeting, and in return for the gay and lesbian community's election assistance, Barney promised several things, including the sponsoring of a gay rights bill in the Massachusetts Senate, which he did.

"What is most amazing about that bill is that it turned out as good as it did," said Elaine. "Bob Dowe and myself wrote it late one evening. Technically, we barely knew what we were doing, but it was a lot of fun. We used stacks of law books for reference, and lifted entire passages which other minorities had previously written in pursuit of their own civil rights. We noticed that the law books often referred to 'public accommodation.' 'What's that?' I asked Bob. 'I don't know,' he frankly admitted, 'but other civil rights bills always have it, so let us have it too!' Funny? Okay. But that's how it was done. Fifteen years later, a direct descendant of our bill is getting close to being passed into law!"

When Barney was seeking election to the United States House of Representatives, Ann began making very positive political suggestions to Elaine. "There's going to be an open seat in Massachusetts' House of Representatives in 1974," she said. "Why don't you run for it?"

An incredulous look appeared on Elaine's face. "Me?" she responded, beginning to articulate a modest protest (although, from the first suggestion, Elaine genuinely favored the idea).

"Sure, why not you?" replied Ann, smiling encouragement. "The old people in your neighborhood will elect you. They don't care if you're a gay woman. They love you! The old folks are your natural constituency. Go home and make a list of all the things you've done for them, and when you've done that, let me take a look at it."

The next day, having followed her mentor's suggestion, Elaine again wanted reassurance that she could win a political campaign. Ann Lewis explained carefully. "A city election would be hard for you to win," she said, "maybe impossible. Citywide, homophobia would kill you. But state elections are different. They are not statewide. They are not even citywide in dense population areas like Boston. Legislators for Massachusetts' House of Representatives are chosen from carefully drawn, limited areas of population. It so happens that your neighborhood, Fenway, makes up more than half the votes from one of those districts. The rest is rich Back Bay Boston. It makes for a crazy mix, and it'll take work to get the votes, but you can do it!"

Elaine sighed thoughtfully.

"If you have any doubts," Ann continued, "remember, people have a liking for you, they've learned to trust you, and you've fought for them. You've been doing things over the years like what a politician does for people who vote for him. Only you've never been paid! Would you be opposed to getting a paycheck? Why shouldn't you be elected?"

Elaine grinned. "Okay, let's do it," she said with a twinkle in her eyes.

"It was a bloody, terrible campaign," the candidate vividly remembered. "All over the country the newspapers, radio, and television began talking about the lesbian that was running for office, and the publicity was picked up by my opponent, who said I had become a national gay personality and would never again pay attention to local constituents. At every turn, being a lesbian was used against me. There was one woman who lived on Queensbury Street who frequently came where I was speaking and tried to hit me with her umbrella while shouting nothing but 'Sodom and Gomorrah' over and over and over.

"Whenever there was a 'Candidates' Night,' one of my primary opponents, a wife-mother politician with large jowls and too many teeth, always belabored an obvious antigay position by placing her husband and children on display. Before long, as a countermeasure, I began bringing my Welsh terrier with me to political meetings. For several evenings, after the wife-mother's saccharine family introductions, I presented my trustworthy dog to the audience. 'Dylan's a beloved part of my home,' I would say sweetly. 'He's five years old, he won't make much noise, and he has one attribute my opponent hasn't yet claimed for her household—Dylan is housebroken.' Of course, everyone in the audience immediately began screaming with laughter, and eventually the other candidate stopped bringing her husband and children. That was fair. After all, they weren't running for office.

"There was also harassment—which never quit! It started as soon as I'd announced for office. Anonymous people seriously threatened to injure me. My homosexuality was their primary preoccupation.

"The first deviltry was sugar in my Chevvy's gas tank. Fortunately, Fenway Joe, a street-smart alcoholic character who lived in my district, had told me important things I should check *before* starting my car. I made the inspection a ritual, and sure enough, one morning I found traces of sugar on the ground near the gas intake. My car had to be towed to a garage and have the fuel tank removed. That was expensive, but if the engine had been used first, it would have been ruined.

"Another time, I was driving toward the University of Massachusetts accompanied by Virginia Hurley, director of the Fenway Community Center, which I'd begun in my district. 'Stop the car!' Virginia suddenly insisted, 'I hear a rattling ping that doesn't sound good.' I slowed down, and we pulled into the nearest gas station. 'Check the tires,' one of us told an attendant. When the man pulled off the hubcaps, he discovered that lug nuts holding the wheels on had all been unscrewed! Some were already loose and had been bouncing around, making the noise. 'If you had driven any faster or any farther,' said the fellow at the station, 'the wheels would have come off of this car. Is somebody trying to kill you?'

"A few days later, my automobile lights were smashed out with a baseball bat. After that, I began hiding the car.

"On several occasions while I was driving, motorists pulled up behind me and intentionally hit the back of my vehicle. Thump—bang—crash! It was frightening. Sometimes I could get license plate numbers, which I referred to the police, but they didn't give me any significant help. I could only hang on and hope that once the election was over, the continually increasing violence would end."

As election day neared, a local Catholic priest saw fit to write an open letter declaring that any of his people who campaigned or voted for Elaine would be excommunicated! That statement was cause for consternation in poor but religious Fenway. Noble recalled, "One of my spry Irish ladies came running up to me with the priest's homophobic political paper in hand. 'Elaine, Elaine,' the woman said, 'look at this, my dear. Now they're telling all them at the Center that we're gonna be excommunicated if we work for ya! Indeed, I don't think it's true, but I have to confess I'm just a little bit frightened.'"

Elaine carried the letter to Father Tom Oddo, the founder of Dignity, a gay Catholic organization, and placed it in Oddo's hands. "Tom, here's a problem," Elaine said. After reading the other Catholic priest's letter, Father Oddo responded on stationery from Harvard's School of Divinity. He wrote to those who were being intimidated, and he stated how much Elaine Noble had already done for their district, that he knew her to be a fine person, and that she most certainly was a child of God!

Elaine immediately photocopied and began distributing twenty thousand copies of Father Oddo's letter. When Elaine's "dear Irish lady" read the priest's response, she was thoroughly relieved that her soul was not in danger. So impressed was she, in fact, that she took a stack of Father Oddo's rebuttal letter and personally began leafleting. Her first stop was the rectory on Commonwealth Avenue. The dour priest who had threatened Catholic voters with excommunication came to the door. Elaine's spry Irish advocate didn't even say hello to him. She said adamantly, "Here, Father, you look at this!" When he had finished reading, she said, "How do you like that?" and she added, "Do you know what else, Father? In nineteen hundred and nine, when we came over on the boat from County Cork, we lassies slept six and seven in the bed. Just what do you think of that, Father?" And again without waiting for a reply, she returned to the busy sidewalk and made certain the priest could see her handing out additional copies of Father Oddo's letter.

Election Day 1974 finally arrived and was the usual letdown. There was not much more a candidate could do. Gay Americans waited by their radios and television sets for the first results. Elaine busied herself by fretting that her campaign office was getting no calls from the "oldsters," whom she expected would be requesting rides to the polls. "My constituency isn't voting," thought Elaine, "I have done what I could, been through hell, and lost the election." Then, late in the afternoon, as Noble's precinct officers were being relieved of duties and were returning to their election office, they all began relating similar stories. Senior citizens were arriving individually at their polling places in cars operated by Elaine's opponents. As they passed Elaine's people, each elderly voter would whisper privately into the election worker's ear, "Tell Elaine to save her gas. We know there's a shortage, so we're taking our rides from the opposition. But we're not voting for them. We're voting for her! Be sure and tell Elaine not to worry!"

In the final count, Elaine took 59 percent of all votes cast (1,730 to 1,201). This would increase to an astounding 80 percent (3,433 to 869) when she ran for reelection in 1976.

School busing for purposes of integration was a major problem in Boston in 1975, Elaine's first year as a member of Massachusetts' House of Representatives. With her fair skin, blue eyes, and Scotch-Irish ancestry, Elaine

physically looked like a person predisposed to side with
the Irish of South Boston, who strongly opposed busing;
but because of her background and her own firsthand
appreciation of what being bused out of Natrona had accomplished in her own behalf, Elaine supported blacks
who were seeking something better for their children.

Accompanied by one or two members of Boston's citywide Education Coalition, Elaine went, before dawn on
many occasions, into neighborhoods seething with anger.
They tried to calm furious parents, black or white, who
were losing sleep and constantly ready to explode; but
about every ten days racial passion boiled over no matter
what attempts were made to prevent it. White teenagers,
their parents, and people out of work would force dangerous confrontations with blacks. Calling themselves the
"antibusing league," a white majority would surround
schools, demolish buses, and break windows. People
would be injured. On one occasion, the antibusers attacked a black businessman and smashed the bridge of
his nose with the staff of an American flag!

Elaine was part of a group that periodically accompanied black children on buses or, in emergencies, located
black parents and assisted them by escorting their kids
from school if it was dangerous to remain. Not long after
Elaine's election, police were having difficulty restraining
mobs at a besieged school when Elaine and several others
were summoned to the scene. The group was standing
near a police squad car, close to the worsening turmoil,
when a woman beside Elaine shouted, "Gun!"

Everybody dove for cover. "They hit the pavement and
crawled under the squad car," Elaine remembers. "It was
pure panic! I was so frozen with fear, I couldn't move.
All I could do was stand there and look up at the second
story of a rundown residence across the street. A four-

teen-year-old boy, half-hidden by a lace curtain, was braced in a window with a .22 rifle pointed at my head.

"That rifle looked immense as I stared along the barrel into his eyes. Hot perspiration broke out all over my body. I couldn't help but resent the inhumanity that had planted some monstrous idea in the boy's brain. Did he have heroic delusions? Was the gun loaded? Would he pull the trigger?

"Finally, after twenty seconds that seemed forever, a busy, no-nonsense motorcycle cop with red hair glanced in our direction. Seeing people cowering under a squad car should raise anyone's level of adrenaline, so I give that burly officer credit for being calm when nobody else was. Totally disregarding the possibility of his needing cover, he immediately strode toward the house where the boy's heavyset Irish mother, oblivious to everything that was happening, was gossiping over her picket fence. With some irritation, the cop cupped his hand to his mouth and forcibly shouted up at the house, 'Hey you, boy—put that weapon away and get back in there—now!'

"As though awakening from a trance, the young fellow withdrew from the window. The policeman turned to the mother, who was finally watching. 'My James is a good boy!' she declared to the officer.

"'Sure,' answered the unimpressed cop, 'but you see that the rifle gets put away.' With a nod, the woman went inside, and the officer returned to other business. I could hardly believe it was over.

"Within minutes, the superintendent of police arrived, and we jumped in his car. As he gunned his motor and drove away through crowds on the sidewalk, I asked, 'Are we leaving without the kids?'

"'They were taken out from the back,' the harried superintendent said. 'They're gone already—they're safe.'

"So why were we there?"
"We had been used as decoys."

Hazing makes the freshman year difficult for legislators. A woman seeking entry into what once was an exclusively male domain finds acceptance more difficult to obtain than it is for men. Being a lesbian adds fuel to the fire!

Elaine Noble would sit listening to debate in the Massachusetts legislature's hallowed halls and, from the undisguised voices of her colleagues a row or two away, hear comments like "Lesbians stink" or "Queers eat horse puckey." One overbearingly offensive man with a nasty leer said to Elaine, "You haven't made your first speech yet—when you gonna break your maiden?" To which Elaine replied, "I don't know, Representative—when was it you broke your gonads?" The man's eyes widened with surprise, and he turned away, irritated. "She's a hostile woman!" Elaine overheard him complain.

Months passed with more of the same. To lesbian friends Elaine confided, "I don't want to go back inside that place. I can't go back inside." But every day she said to herself, "You have to!"

Elaine quickly realized she was in a war, and many battles remained to be fought. "I never worked so hard in my life," she admitted. "First of all, to keep from losing my mind. Second, to keep from punching somebody in the nose. Third, while taking abuse, to appear ladylike and keep smiling in the face of it!"

Life on the home front offered little respite. Elaine has harrowing memories. "I met Rita before my election, and afterward she came to live with me, but she couldn't take what was happening. People were literally shooting bullets through our windows, destroying our home. Rita had an Audi that she parked on Marlborough Street in front of our brownstone. Men came driving down the street, and they blew out the Audi's back window and the two side windows with a shotgun. Then they stopped, reloaded, leaned out of their vehicle, and blew away the front window. Shattered glass was all over the place. It was at eight o'clock in the morning.

"I asked a neighbor, 'Did you see what was happening?'"

"He said, 'Yes, a man shot the car.'"

"Weeks later, after the Audi had been repaired, the same thing happened all over again. It was horrible. And there were threatening phone calls. Rita was very frightened. She'd had enough and moved away.

"A friend came to visit one evening. In the morning we discovered her car badly scratched. The word 'pervert' was painted on the side.

"A woman who had worked on my campaign lived about a block away. In her brand-new car, somebody planted an explosive device. The blast rocked our entire neighborhood. That was in the middle of the night. No one was hurt, but the car was totally destroyed."

On many occasions, Elaine was asked, "Why can't you do something? You're an elected official. Don't you have some clout?"

She could only attempt to explain. "The police say we have to catch people in the act," she said. "Also remember, to the policemen, not only was I 'queer,' but I had also sided with the blacks on the matter of busing. Consequently, law enforcement was not particularly helpful. In Boston, there are some Irish cops who are gay, and everybody knows it, but they aren't out yet.

"I went to Attorney General Frank Bellotti for help. He was the only official to show any real interest. He worked with me night and day when he could be of assistance, and at the end of my second year in office, in an effort to catch the nuts, Bellotti obtained a private detective to work with me. Three days was all it took for the detective to round up some of the culprits! Can you imagine? He did alone in seventy-two hours what all of Boston's finest couldn't seem to accomplish in a hundred and four weeks? As it turned out, the persons apprehended had lots of money but no Social Security numbers. That indicated the scoundrels were on the payroll of some well-connected folks who didn't want to be identified."

When the Gay Rights Bill came up for a vote in the House of Representatives, a member of Boston's legislative clique passed the word, "Noble doesn't believe in what we believe in. She stood with the blacks. So I'm urging all of you who do not believe in busing to make sure that you don't vote for the Gay Rights Bill. That will teach her!"

"Some of those legislators were pretty jerky," Elaine explained later. "They tried to make me believe that if I'd been in favor of segregation, they might have supported gay rights, but I have to question the validity of that. It's not easy to imagine racists voting for gay people!

"Nevertheless, I always tried to play fair and according to the rules. When an ethics committee was being appointed to specify acceptable codes of conduct for our House of Representatives, I went to the Speaker and asked to be part of the committee. I thought it would be wonderful for people to say, 'That lesbian is an ethical person.' It was, therefore, a disappointment to learn that when the Speaker did appoint me, the result was that he found himself being picketed by his own constituency!"

Elaine Noble has never failed to stir up controversy—which she accomplished simply by being herself, fair and honest. Like the Speaker of the House, Elaine's greatest frustration came from her own people. "After my reelection to a second two-year term of office," she explained, "everybody, nationally and locally, placed constantly increasing demands upon me, demands I could not fulfill. I attended as many gay meetings as I could. I was out almost every night. But I had to balance my time between national homosexual organizations that did not elect me and the nongay residents and neighborhood ladies who did. When you are the first of anything, everyone has his or her own separate image of how you should be and what you should do. It's impossible to satisfy everybody. For me, the result was that a vocal minority from the local gay community became exceedingly spiteful even though I had always walked the extra mile for gay people, and made no bones about it!

"What I wanted most, more than life itself, was passage of our Gay Rights Bill in Massachusetts. Its outlook for success was very promising during my fourth year in office. Bringing gay rights into law was to be my ultimate legislative act! To aid in its accomplishment, I had saved up all the goodwill my nongay colleagues owed me. For the first time ever, everybody in leadership positions, including the Speaker and the Minority Leader, voted for the bill! Still, there were not enough votes for passage."

So, how did the bill fail?

This is the sad part of the story.

During the morning before the vote, a small, wealthy group of self-appointed gay individuals who were concerned with their own agendas and piqued by Elaine's growing popularity, went to the Republicans. They said, "We are uncertain about our support for Elaine's strategy. We think it might be best if you take the Gay Rights Bill away from her."

"You mean you want us to vote against it?" asked an incredulous politician.

"For right now, yes," replied the unrepresentative delegation of political dabblers, with little thought or understanding of how they were squandering Elaine's careful accumulation of political favors. Nor did they have any idea how quickly their suggestion would be seized upon by politicians who had no inherent desire to pass a gay rights bill, then or ever.

The result was a calamity.

Within an hour Elaine's delicate advantage evaporated. "We were intending to go out on a limb and vote for your bill," some Republican legislators told her, "but some influential gay men came to us and said to vote against it. It was crazy. Do you know how jealous they are of you? So much that we are going to give them a lesson. We have changed our minds. We are not going to vote for gay rights. And you can tell those elite friends of yours that it will be a cold day in hell when we do!'"

Blood drained from Elaine's face.

"Oh, no! Please don't do that!" she pleaded.

Elaine had worked hard to utilize the political system, delivering a high quality of service to her constituents and earning deserved respect in a very tight club. Other politicians may not have approved of Elaine's sexuality, but after working shoulder-to-shoulder with her in tough legislative sessions, they could not help but become close. Elaine had reason to be hopeful when she reached for her colleagues' hearts and begged with soulful passion, "Please, please stand with me on this!"

But it was too late. The Republicans said, "No. We've changed our minds. Those people of yours have lost our vote!"

By the end of the day, spoilers of the gay bill realized their mistake. The small, well-dressed group went to Elaine's office, presumably repentant and sorry to have interfered in a world of political realities. One of them carried twelve long-stemmed roses. When he proffered the elegant flowers, he said, "We're sorry. We goofed, and we know we goofed."

Elaine stared in disbelief at the delegation. She was in no mood for apologies. Forgiveness was not compatible with what she was thinking.

"There they were," she said later. "They wanted to tell me that they were so sorry. And they were acting like it could all be made okay with a dozen roses!" But she knew the mischief done that day would last a long time, and it would not soon be made okay. The damage was real.

"You will not have an opportunity—not for many years—to get this bill as far as I could have gotten it to-day," Elaine passionately declared. "It wasn't only me that got hurt. You have prevented every homosexual in Massachusetts from having a gay civil rights bill now because of negative behavior. Negative is not what the gay community is. If you don't know what we are about, I'll tell you. It's called winning!"

Elaine's damaged pride fused with a burning anger. Neither would soon be dissipated. Those emotions, coupled with the bitter burden of a failure that had come so close to success, were factors influencing her decision not to stand for reelection.

As for the small group of men from whom Elaine refused to accept roses, they were invited, in no uncertain terms, to remove their bright flowers, their sad apologies, and themselves forever from her presence. Co-workers and political friends, who were tired of seeing Elaine take abuse, applauded as the rebuked offenders retreated from the office.

Elaine managed a grin, and from out of the pain came a bit of Irish laughter. "Thank you," she said to the stal-

wart gay people who remained. "Politics is a nutty business. It makes you crazy in the head. I don't think
anybody should have to do it all of their adult life!"

Elaine, still vitally involved in politics, helping others to
succeed on the same trail she blazed, observed, "Being
the first, and the only, was difficult. I was not prepared
for the demands, and that was really tough. But being
the first and only cuts both ways. There were also a lot
of nice things that happened.

"It felt good when I would read a letter, or people
would call me late at night with their stories, and they'd
say I gave them a sense of hope. Then I'd read about
how gay people all over America were beginning to realize there was progress they could make in their own political backyards. That idea spread in all directions,
expanding like circular ripples in a pond. It made me
feel really great!

"I helped raise money for Karen Clark, an elected State
Representative in Minnesota. She came to a workshop I
did in Vermont, and she said, "You talked to me about
running. Perhaps you don't remember, but that's what
made me make a decision to go home and campaign.

"Alan Spears, another successful politician and a dear
man, said, 'You gave me the guts to come out.'

"David Scondras now has my old Fenway District in
Boston. If he gets into political trouble, I do what I can
to help. We get together and fix it. Today, there is a gay
liaison in the office of the Mayor of Boston.

"That is the good part—getting involved with some
very nice people. I love the gay community, and I care."

A Mack Truck Is Coming and You'd Better Get Out of the Way

Gay Pride patterned itself on Black Pride—with a difference: White homosexuals were not usually objects of discrimination within the boundaries of their own gay community; black homosexuals, on the other hand, often found no refuge anywhere, and sometimes had to make unpleasant choices. Living in communities of their racial heritage, openly gay blacks faced cruel rejection; living in predominantly white gay communities, racism was a fact of life. Coming out of the closet frequently meant "damned if you do—damned if you don't" for people of color. Sometimes it became hard to take, being a "nigger" to homosexual whites and a "faggot" to heterosexual blacks!

It is not commendable that a community born of suffering and reared with harsh insensitivity by a prejudiced majority should replicate the wrong. Who would know better than gay people that any intolerance, gay or non-gay, black or white, causes too much pain and anger?

"We must begin to speak of our love and our concern for each other," wrote Joseph Beam, gay editor of *In the Life,* a best-selling black anthology.

Dr. Alfred N. Gerald, an official of the World Health Organization and a citizen of Panama, was no stranger to discrimination. When his black wife, American-born in New York City, was pregnant, there were two options: the indignity of childbirth involving a less-than-equal attitude toward treatment of blacks within the United States Canal Zone, or childbirth at a nondiscriminatory hospital in the surrounding Republic of Panama. Adamantly displeased by the injustice of segregation, Dr. Gerald would not allow his wife's delivery at the Canal facilities. Therefore, their newborn son, Gilberto, was born in Panama instead of on territory of the United States, and consequently would not automatically be entitled to American citizenship. (Also, an unanticipated technicality existed involving Gil's mother. Unlike males, female United States citizens in 1950 were required—in order to pass citizenship on to their children—to have resided for a specific period of time within the United States after the age of eighteen. Gil's mother did not meet this requirement.) Nevertheless, in 1967, after grammar school in Panama and high school elsewhere, and having traveled throughout the Caribbean, the Americas, and in Africa, Gilberto chose to emigrate from Trinidad and Tobago to the United States. His youngest brother, unencumbered by their mother's residency requirement (which she had fulfilled by the time he was born), automatically became an American citizen. That same citizenship would eventually become a problem for Gilberto. In the meantime, merely entering the country of his mother and brothers was not difficult. Gil, as yet unaware of his sexuality, was obviously healthy and full of energy. He was not big. His features were fine, and his bright eyes were windows of intelligence.

Gilberto enrolled at Pratt Institute in Brooklyn to study architecture. "I always wanted to be an architect," he said, "since I was a kid of four or five. My parents were having a new home built in the suburbs of Panama about the time I was ready to begin kindergarten. We were living in an apartment in the meantime, and when the adults had finished poring over house plans spread on our dining-room table, they let me look at them too. From the beginning, I understood how bits and pieces of construction go together to make an attractive building.

"We made trips to the work site, and with some help from my father, I easily made the connection between plans on paper and their three-dimensional counterpart rising from a concrete foundation. From then on, even during recess periods in grade school, I spent many hours drawing my own original plans for houses, or altering those that I found in *House & Garden* and other American magazines."

The waiting period prior to eligibility for citizenship in the United States is five years, the same length of time required for a degree in architecture at Pratt. Gil was a third-year student, president of his fraternity, and dating a female art major when his world changed forever.

It happened during "rush" week, when prospective pledges are invited to fraternity houses and screened for membership. While piano music was played in the Tau Delta Phi living room, two male college sophomores, who were present for the first time, began playfully dancing together. After some beer, and warming to not-so-innocent kidding, they pulled each other closer and closer. With barely disguised sexual overtones, joined at the waist, they waltzed around the floor.

"I remember thinking," said Gilberto, "they're not going to get an invitation to join Tau Delta Phi—but they did. A few nights afterward, late in the evening, I was alone in my room working over a drawing board when one of the two, a tall, slender fellow, came into my room and sat at my desk.

"While I fussed with an architectural detail, he said, 'I would like to thank you as fraternity president for the invitation to join, but I can't. I know you understand. The others, they wouldn't be comfortable with somebody like me around.'"

Pretending not to understand, Gilberto asked for an explanation, but was not prepared for the matter-of-fact reply. "I'm gay," said the tall fellow, and Gil, very startled, jerked his body upright and literally fell off his stool! He was thoroughly shocked that anyone could possibly live so comfortably with the idea of being homosexual. He had never conceived that any human being would simply admit to being "queer"—without torture or getting caught in the act.

"You're what?" Gilberto heard himself attempt to whisper in a voice that seemed overly loud. When his visitor dutifully began to repeat the word "gay," Gil did three things almost simultaneously. He struggled to get up from the floor, involuntarily reached to stop the other man's lips, and rushed for the door of his room, which he slammed shut.

"What a jolt!" Gil recalled. "I'd never imagined such a situation—but his presence was a blessing. In a sense, he was the first life preserver that had ever been thrown at me. I grabbed for the sanity of what he had to say! There was no use lying to myself anymore. He had seen my side glances and realized I was living a lie. With my secret out, suddenly, I no longer wanted to deny who I was. My heart began to beat like a jackhammer!

"'There's no point in fooling yourself,' said my visitor. 'You only cause a lot of damage.' Several days later he introduced me to a disco, where I discovered that other gay people existed. What a favor he did, providing my first glimpse into the real gay world. I don't remember his name. We were never very close. It's no joke when I say I owe so much to a tall, handsome stranger."

Gilberto was distressed by the war in Vietnam and worked against it. With even greater vigor, he explored the gay and lesbian community—and discovered anger within himself directed at all the energy he felt he had wasted during the confusing years when he was still uncertain of his own sexual identity.

"Nobody should have to go through that," Gil said. "Learning only by chance that gay is okay. Finding out the hard way that gay people are healthy and making key contributions to society. I don't think any young homosexual person should have to spend five unnecessary minutes feeling lonely and facing rejection. A person who is homosexual should be able to go forward in life. And take that life to its maximum potential!"

Gil never doubted that God loved gay people. "Troy Perry was the first person to affirm that to me," he said, "but my problem never was in accepting myself. The fear I had was something different. I was afraid of losing friends, and I was extremely afraid of family rejection!"

Gilberto's father had numerous virtues. Dr. Gerald was a caring, loving parent. He worked to provide the best of everything for his family, sending all four sons to college. Nevertheless, there was valid reason for apprehension. Although the good doctor had never been overtly demonstrative, there were strong indications that he could be unpleasantly rigid in maintaining certain ideas. In particular, it was evident that he would never support the idea of any of his sons being homosexual!

"I built up the courage to tell my mother," said Gilberto, "and she shared the information with my father. He was on an assignment in South America at the time, but by mail and telephone they decided to send me for psychological help. Predictably, the treatment was ineffectual.

"For a considerable time afterwards, my father denied there was any truth to my being homosexual. He had no patience for the suggestion of "perversion" and—after initial conversations—made it clear to everyone that he never wanted to be reminded of it again.

"My first lover was a special person. I naively thought my father would think better of gay people after meeting him, and would come to realize that the stereotypes he envisioned were generally unreal. Unfortunately, when my father realized what kind of relationship existed between my lover and myself, it was instantly apparent I was mistaken. There were awful moments of tension before my father finally said, 'Your friend's okay. I think he's a nice person. But don't ever bring him around here again! I don't want to be reminded of how I failed.'

"My anger was internalized by the comment. I didn't say much. If my father was hurt, I, in turn, was devastated by his rejection of such an inherently important, nonescapable part of my being. He said, 'I think you are ninety-nine percent perfect—let's not throw the other one percent up in my face!' The only trouble with his percentages was that they weren't valid. My sexuality is a vitally important part of myself, and his pretending otherwise was not only unscientific, but for me, distressing in the extreme.

"I decided at that time to abide by his terms. In no way would I intentionally remind him again of the sexual aspect of my life. The sad result, however, was that it set us apart, shut us off from each other. His terms meant that when holidays came—the Fourth of July, Thanksgiving, birthdays, anniversaries, Christmas, and Easter—I had to choose with whom I would spend the time, my family or my lover. It was always tormenting, and always my family came up on the short end of the stick. I was not going to leave my lover alone and cause him unhappiness so that Dad would not be reminded of who I am.

"Basically, my father's rigid inability to cope with his sexual prejudice meant that when I needed him most, he and my family would no longer be an integral part of my life. My private tears would dry on a pillow in the dark of night, but I had to come to terms with that. It is terrible to be close yet hopelessly separated from people who love you, people you care so much about.

"My mother tried to heal the breach. Sometimes she would go shopping with my lover and try to get him to reason with me to work out an understanding with my father. That was futile. Try as best I could, there was only continuing pain for both of us. There was even a time I tried to use religion to salve the wound. I asked my mother and father to come to Metropolitan Community Church, where I had become a member of the Board of Directors. My mother attended on several occasions. But my father refused and said to me, 'I don't care if Jesus Christ was gay, I think you're all sick! And I'll die thinking you're sick!'

"For the good of no one, he probably will.

"Eventually there came a day when I concluded I needed to limit my anger, needed to remember I'm an adult in full command of my faculties and should be respected for making my own decisions. I knew that not only was I not bad, my life was fulfilling and happy outside of the sphere of paternal influence. There was nothing I had done I wouldn't do again. It was a shame for all of us that we were unable to share our daily triumphs of living. But in spite of the shadow cast by my father's disapproval, it was not the end of my life."

Gilberto Gerald was graduated from Pratt Institute's School of Architecture in 1974. The following year, his application for American citizenship was unsuccessful because of bureaucratic error. Three years later, when Gil reapplied for citizenship, a serious new barrier existed: Gil's homosexual lifestyle. He had become openly gay during the critical intervening years.

Called for a routine interview by the Immigration and Naturalization Service in 1979, Gil obtained the best advice available, then made his own decision on how to proceed. He could either perjure himself by lying about his homosexuality or risk repeated rejection for telling the truth.

If Gilberto lied and was caught, he would surely be turned away, and intentional omissions of fact on an application for citizenship are considered no better than falsehoods. Gilberto decided to tell the truth—the whole truth. He was convinced he wanted to become a citizen "without a cloud" always over his head. Consequently, when Gil was asked on the application for citizenship to list organizations with which he was affiliated, he boldly wrote:

1. National Coalition of Black Gays
2. Metropolitan Community Church

And as if that declaration wasn't being honest enough, when asked to bring two people with him to support his statement of fitness to become a citizen, the people he chose were his lover of three years and a gay friend.

Predictably, the interviewer was not pleased. He arched his eyebrows in classic fashion, peering with severity at Gilberto, who sweltered in his own bravado. "Am I reading this right?" asked the incredulous interviewer.

"I would expect so," answered Gilberto, irritated that his excellent knowledge of English, American History, and Civics was not reason enough for his speedy naturalization.

Quite to the contrary, the interviewer frowned, and asked, "What do these organizations you belong to mean? Are you a homosexual?"

"Yes," replied Gil, showing annoyance.

"Jesus!" snapped the government man. "Do you realize there's an unresolved public debate about homosexuality in this country? That it's impossible for anybody to be accepted if there's evidence of moral turpitude. You should withdraw your application—everybody might be better off!"

Gilberto verbally expressed his anger.

The government shelved his application.

As a result, Gil's quest for citizenship lay dormant again, this time until the summer of 1980, when it became apparent Jimmy Carter would not be reelected. "If Ronald Reagan becomes President, conservative intolerance in Washington, D.C., will unquestionably be in ascendance," Gil reasoned; and since homophobia might finally destroy any chance of his being naturalized, he decided that without delay, a last-ditch effort should be mounted before Carter was ousted.

He called the Immigration and Naturalization Service regularly, getting nowhere as he attempted to resurrect his application. Precious time had been squandered. Now time was inexorably ticking away!

Attempts to obtain help, or even a response, from Wal-

ter Fauntroy, a Baptist minister, and the District of Columbia's black delegate to Congress, were futile. The
Congressman did not take Gilberto's telephone calls, nor
did he answer his letters.

A full year later, there was still little progress. Winter
had come, blossomed into spring, and deteriorated into a
typically humid summer. Reagan was President, and civil
rights leaders were already beginning to despair for reasons of their own. Frustrated, Gilberto acquiesced to legal
advice and firmly demanded that the government take
action on the application without further delay one way
or the other! Mike Maggio, Gil's able attorney, was successful in persuading the reticent bureaucracy to grant
one final interview.

Gilberto's mother insisted upon accompanying her son
to face what they expected might be a difficult inquisition.
Mrs. Gerald, provoked, could probably tap a reserve of
maternal eloquence to overwhelm nearly anyone attempting to confound Gilberto. Mama's opinion was that it
was time the Immigration and Naturalization Service listened, and learned something positive about gay people!

But there was no interview.

At the last possible minute, the government man decided to meet only with Maggio, and gave the lawyer detailed instructions and helpful hints as to how to proceed
further. An affidavit was suggested, delineating Gilberto's
attributes and good character and making legal arguments for his admission. It was (and still is) illegal for
known gay persons to immigrate into the United States.
However, Gilberto's entry was not illegal for the simple
reason that he honestly did not realize he was homosexual until after gaining admission. It is not illegal for a
homosexual of good character—who is *already* a legal resident—to be given citizenship; *but* the determination is

left to federal judges, who rule differently depending upon their own thinking and upon the state or district where their jurisdiction is located. Every case is complicated with individual legal grounds and precedents, and there are no promises.

In the affidavit to Immigration and Naturalization, Gilberto never wavered in his determination to become an American citizen without any false pretenses. He wrote, "I am an active member of several organizations devoted to the welfare of the community, such as Metropolitan Community Church and the National Coalition of Black Gays. Since reaching an awareness of my homosexual identity, I have always felt healthy and normal regarding that aspect of my personality. I seek to become a full citizen of the United States."

In January of 1982, Gilberto Gerald, having been determined by the Immigration and Naturalization Service to be a wholesome human being, a civic-minded person, and a homosexual—with a favorable ruling by Judge June Green—was sworn and declared a citizen of the United States of America. During an impressive ceremony with a group at the U.S. District Court House in Washington, D.C., Gilberto recited the Oath of Allegiance, sang "The Star-Spangled Banner," and received the gift of a small American flag from a delegation of the Daughters of the American Revolution.

While struggling to become a citizen, Gil found some success as an architect. The only marring element was that sometimes racism intruded. Too often, Gil overheard remarks in large business offices that brought his blood to a boil. Before long, he determined he would not be the object of discrimination because of either his sex or color, neither of which was his to choose.

"I recall sitting in my office," said Gilberto, "hearing other architects say the vilest things imaginable about homosexuals, and having to remain silent—from fear. Eventually, I revolted against that. I left an important assignment, vowing that I'd never again be in a situation where I would have to worry about what could happen to me for confronting someone who proved to be a rotten excuse for a civilized person.

"The next time I got hired, I listed all the gay associations I had, relevant or not. I did it because my pride was valuable to me, and because the next time my lover called, I didn't want to have to whisper into the phone or play untruthful little games. When the Mayor appointed a committee to develop the Comprehensive Plan for the District of Columbia, I was appointed to be one of the architects, not only because of my professional reputation but also because, politically, I openly represented the gay and lesbian community.

"I could never separate the oppression of being a gay man from that which I feel being a black man," continued Gil. "Think of it this way. If there is a door, and a sign over the door says 'No Blacks and No Queers Admitted,' and you take off the 'No Blacks' part of the sign, or you take off the 'No Queers' part of the sign, I'm still hung up by one or the other. I'm left outside in either case.

"Both signs are wrong.

"Within the gay and lesbian community, too often the argument has been that we can't divide our energies—we have to concentrate on getting just the 'queer' signs down because some of us are undecided about the 'black' signs, and worrying about that will make us less effective. Well, that's a cop-out. Because when that 'queer' sign does come down (and I have worked to get that 'queer' sign down), I fear the white 'queers' will go through the door, lock it from inside, and I'll be the black 'queer' left out—more alone than ever."

As a result of apprehension and experience, Gilberto became part of a new organization formed by black gay men and black lesbians to uncover and promote their own history, to fight racism, and to expose pervasive homophobia within the black community. "When the media have photographed or reported on the gay movement," said Gil, "they have repeatedly selected the whites of Castro Street and Greenwich Village, forgetting that homosexuals comprise ten percent of *all* the world's population, and that people of color are an important part of our very diverse gay community. The media's limited vision causes many to lose sight of the numbers of people we are dealing with, and diminishes a universal perception of the breadth, wealth, and enormous strength of gay communities.

"Our black coalition commenced in 1978 when Marion Barry was first running for Mayor in the District of Columbia. I was beginning to become interested in politics, and found myself dismayed. Washington, D.C., has a population that is three-quarters black, and consequently it followed that three-quarters of the resident homosexuals in Washington, D.C., would also be black—but the gay political muscle was entirely white!

"Therefore, when a man named Billy Jones placed an advertisement in one of the gay magazines revealing that there were others as concerned as myself, and that a black political group was being formed, it was the spark I needed. I immediately embraced the idea. A few of us met, and thus was born what evolved into the National Coalition of Black Lesbians and Gays. I was finally able to politically integrate my gay identity and my black identity. No longer did I have to divorce the gay being from the black being. It was possible to meet oppression with a united front.

"An apartment sufficed for our first meeting, but before long, people in cities beyond our immediate area also showed interest, and we became a movement. During the first year of existence we met with representatives of President Carter's administration. We also organized the first National Third World Lesbian and Gay Conference, which was held simultaneously with the 1979 Gay and Lesbian March on Washington. Our Coalition's objective has always embodied an emphasis on the black and the gay identity—that you can be proud of both without separation. Coming to terms with the two communities has long been a key issue with me, and so it remains.

"I have been accused, unrightly from my perspective, of expecting more from the gay community than from the black community. In point of fact, I have found occasions when it has been necessary to tackle both.

"The black community, with centuries of unjustified mistreatment notwithstanding, has been widely insensitive to its own homosexual minority. But our gay community is something new. In many ways, it grew out of the black civil rights upheaval. At this moment in history, our movement is an infant in the universal span of time—about a score of years measured in memorable human terms. Insensitivity in the gay community cannot be excused by pointing toward similar inequities in established black or white communities. We have an opportunity to do something better!"

"I still have a dream," declared Martin Luther King, Jr., at the rally concluding the March on Washington for Jobs and Freedom that took place on August 28, 1963. "It is a dream deeply rooted in the American dream,"

King said. "I have a dream that one day this nation will rise up and live out the true meaning of its creed, 'We hold these truths to be self-evident, that all men are created equal.'"

Those memorable words at the steps of the Lincoln Memorial were from the same man who several months before—on an evening preceding the famous antidiscrimination demonstrations in Birmingham, Alabama—had said, "I know when I say don't be afraid, you know what I mean. Don't even be afraid to die. I submit to you tonight that no man is free if he fears death. But the minute you conquer the fear of death, at that moment you are free. You must say somehow, I don't have much money, I don't have much education, I may not be able to read and write, but I have the capacity to die." Five years later, Martin Luther King, Jr., was immortal.

After another fifteen years, a prestigious group designating itself the Coalition of Conscience planned another march to mark the twentieth anniversary of their original March on Washington. The Anniversary March, scheduled for Saturday, August 27, 1983, was intended to be a dynamic reminder of the fallen leader, as well as everything he lived and died for in the civil rights movement. The martyr's widow, Coretta Scott King, would lead the celebration.

Directors of the National Coalition of Black Gays (which became the National Coalition of Black Lesbians and Gays) found endorsement of the new March on Washington to be consistent with their objectives. Gilberto Gerald, executive director of the Coalition, said: "We had no delusions that we were an organization capable of delivering hordes of black, openly gay and lesbian people on the day of the march. We were comparatively small. We merely had in mind that our National Coalition

of Black Gays would gain status by having its name officially included on literature printed for the celebration."
There was not a hint that, as a result of their endorsement, Gilberto would soon face "perhaps the most emotionally challenging task" of his life.

Long before August, conflict began concerning the Anniversary March. On April 29, a press notice was released
by the National Coalition of Black Gays to the effect that
it was proud to be the first gay or lesbian organization to
endorse the 1983 march. Other homosexual groups
around the nation, however, were in no hurry. Many
were concerned about the reception they would receive
from Southern Christian organizers and administrators
of the march. They had only a short time to wait. Within
a week, Frank Branchini, staff member of the Gay Rights
National Lobby, telephoned Gilberto.

"You have problems," Frank said.

"Like what?" asked Gil.

"The march doesn't want faggots."

"Surely you're kidding?"

"I wish. It came out when Michelle Guimarin allowed
as how the National Gay Task Force should be included
with other national groups on the march's steering committee. That's when their chief watchdog, Congressman
Fauntroy, who *is* the national chair of the March Administrative Committee, let go his little bombshell. Seems the
Congressman casually indicated something to the effect
that gay rights are about as important as civil rights are
for penguins! That from a person who was an aide to
Martin Luther King. Does it grab you?"

Gilberto felt a sudden sadness. He shook his head, remembering Fauntroy as a preacher-turned-politician who
wouldn't give him even the courtesy of a reply when, as
a black homosexual, he had asked for a little help in his

quest for citizenship. At a later date, Gil reconsidered and concluded, "One cannot say our Congressman has not been supportive. He was a sponsor of the National Gay Rights Bill from the very beginning. It's only that he needs a bit of pushing. I think Walter Fauntroy the Congressman has good civil rights instincts, but Walter Fauntroy the Reverend may have trouble dealing with his religious views."

On Fauntroy's administrative committee for the march, Donna Brazile was the able, hardworking, nuts-and-bolts coordinator with an inside overview of events. Gilberto, still smoldering as a result of the bitter news from Branchini, immediately telephoned Donna. "It's ironic," Gilberto complained. "Bayard Rustin, strategist and de facto organizer of the original March on Washington in 1963, was denounced in Congress by Senator Strom Thurmond for being 'queer,' among other charges. When nervous ministers reacted adversely, Martin Luther King, Jr., himself stood up for Rustin and saved his job. The march went on to be a great success—with lots of credit to a gay man. Yet now, two decades later, we're told our gay presence isn't necessary!"

The conversation waxed warm. Donna, an authoritative woman with a deep voice, was of the opinion that the gay community was still welcome to participate in the Anniversary March despite anything Gilberto had been told. Donna assured Gil that the National Coalition of Black Gays would have its name printed on all future literature concerning the march. "You know, misunderstandings happen," she said. "And if you're looking for historic irony, Gilberto, try this: Twenty years ago they almost forgot to include a woman on the program!"

One month later, in June, the National Gay Task Force, with some apprehension, also endorsed the march, and indicated that the black coalition should handle details of gay black and white participation. However, soon thereafter, Jeff Levi of the Gay Task Force joined Gilberto in a meeting with Donna Brazile. Their ambition was to urge the inclusion of a homosexual speaker when the march ended at the Lincoln Memorial. Writers Audre Lorde and James Baldwin were suggested. Donna could see no difficulty with the idea and promised that at the next meeting of the Coalition of Conscience, which had the last word on marching and speaking arrangements, she would ask for approval.

"I had no doubt Donna would succeed," said Gilberto. "Donna Brazile is a dynamic woman you wouldn't want to mess with."

Nevertheless, it became evident that something was wrong. Telephone calls from Gilberto to Donna's office began to have obviously strained responses, with assistants saying Donna was out, and could they take a message? But calls were not being answered. Before long there was a general realization that although the National Coalition of Conscience had not actually rejected the participation of gay and lesbian groups, neither was there any evidence of welcome.

Time and again, in disbelief, gay men and lesbians across America asked of one another, "How is it possible that a Coalition of Conscience, whose primary theme is "Jobs, Peace and Freedom"—which knows firsthand of all the ill effects of discrimination, and includes in its numbers between two and three million black homosexuals stifled inside their own private closets—will turn its back on a friendly, struggling minority that is taking nothing away from anybody, but seeking only deliverance from unreasonable bigotry?"

In the middle of August, two weeks before the march,

pressure began to build. At the Mt. Zion Baptist Church, a displeased delegation from the District of Columbia's black lesbian and gay community stood and was recognized in the jam-packed last meeting of the local District of Columbia branch of the Coalition of Conscience. Phil Pannell, a black activist, eloquently told the local Coalition of Conscience how a majority of the gay community had supported antidiscriminatory activities in general and the Anniversary March in particular. Then Pannell, backed by the gay delegation, introduced a motion for the local march organization to request of the national organization that it reverse its unspoken decision to pretend twenty-five million people in the United States do not exist.

There was silence in the sultry room for long, droning moments following the speeches, but only the small part of a minute had passed when, unexpectedly, as though an electric current charged the room, bright smiles broke out on hundreds of faces. Approval was by genuine acclamation! Spontaneous applause shook the solid Baptist Church, and cordiality filled the sanctuary. Reverend Gibson, pastor of Mt. Zion, promised to carry the District of Columbia's message to the National Coalition.

Days later, however, there was no sign that the Coalition of Conscience was interested, or had even taken notice. The only news was a shattering rumor that if there was to be a gay marching contingent, it would be scheduled to trail at the end of the parade. Gay people recoiled from such a put-down with something approaching total disbelief. "My God," exclaimed Gilberto, "would they intentionally send us to the back of the goddamn bus!"

Another urgent message was left for Donna Brazile, and when it also went unanswered, Gilberto finally lost patience and left a final statement for the coordinator of the march. "I am forced to declare war on the Coalition of Conscience!" Gilberto told one of her unidentified assistants. When Gil called the media that same day, reporters, including those from the local press and national television, showed considerable interest. Gil told them that the march was unquestionably worthy of support, but problems existed. A boycott was never suggested. The gay community merely wanted to be reasonably included. And yes, because months of unilateral verbal exhortation had been ineffective, a short list of demands would need to be drafted.

In the office of the Georgetown firm where Gil was employed, his work on an architectural design for the enormous Washington Harbor Project went untouched for days. "I began to simply 'work' the phone like a maniac," he wrote. "Oddly enough, my fellow workers did not express any annoyance with me. They seemed somewhat amused and impressed. They were intrigued when TV crews began calling me at the office for interviews. A female colleague of mine remarked that she felt as if she 'was on a movie set.'"

Gilberto began sending Mailgrams to the top national leaders of the Coalition of Conscience. He was determined there should be no doubt that they had been informed. Mailgrams went specifically to Coretta Scott King, Joseph Lowery, Benjamin Hooks, and Walter Fauntroy. The Mailgrams were one long paragraph pleading for the recipients to make viable gay and lesbian participation possible in the march.

Mailgrams were also sent to every national gay and lesbian organization in the United States. Gilberto asked all gay people to swamp Fauntroy's office with correspondence protesting the intransigence of the march chairman. As a result, eight days before the march, a minimum of six major gay organizations were peppering the Congressman's mailbox and telephones with protests, prompting Cliff Roberson, a ward coordinator in the Mayor's office, to warn Fauntroy's administrative assistant that the Congressman would be wise to change his position and to "Move—because a Mack truck is coming, and you'd better get out of the way!"

Behind the scenes, Gilberto was working feverishly with Ginny Apuzzo, executive director of the National Gay Task Force. Together, they maintained pressure on the steering committee of the National Coalition of Conscience. In support of requests from Gilberto and Ginny, Judy Goldsmith, president of the National Organization for Women, made it clear to march leaders that N.O.W. was very seriously considering keeping their huge membership at home if the Coalition of Conscience would not come to an accommodation with the gay community. Asia Bennett, executive director of the American Friends Service Committee (Quakers), together with delegations from Europe, all key members in the Coalition of Conscience, similarly threatened to withdraw.

Fauntroy could not help but be aware of the political buildup. Labor leaders, the Mayor's people, and gays throughout the District of Columbia were part of the machine. At the same time, although a few heterosexuals were wringing their hands, complaining that black gays were being disloyal to their heritage for tarnishing the significance of the march in 1963, truly dedicated people were sincerely torn between issues that needed explaining.

Four days before the march, the National Coalition of Conscience had not softened its position. Gilberto's Mailgrams to them were unanswered. "I believe in the use of demonstrations to further a cause," he said, "but I never thought it would become necessary in dealing with people

I have always deeply admired. In the beginning, my preference was to ask nicely, giving them every opportunity to respond in any reasonable way. But failing that, when we were drowning in our own goodwill, I said, 'Enough! Mobilize the community, and let's really fight!' Which is what we did.

"A series of events took place. The genuine threat to move N.O.W. and the American Friends Service Committee out of the march was a primary factor. It was also important that both Fauntroy and the march began getting negative press in *The Washington Post* and *The Washington Times*. When the Congressman found it necessary to deny his 'penguin rights' statement, we knew the time had arrived to turn up the heat."

On Tuesday, media were alerted that a sit-in at the offices of Congressman Fauntroy would commence Wednesday afternoon, less than three full days before the march. Timing must have been perfect, because the well-considered announcement bore immediate results. Before noon on Wednesday, Donna Brazile called Gilberto for the first time in many weeks. "The Coalition of Conscience wants to speak with you," she said.

"Who on the committee?"

"All the big guns."

"You wouldn't kid me, Donna?"

"Yes, I would—but not about this."

"When'd they arrive?" asked Gil, suddenly awed by the imminence of meeting his living heroes.

"They're not here yet," Donna explained. "It'll be a conference call. You know, connecting lines from half-a-dozen cities—to get this thing settled tonight."

"That suits me," agreed Gilberto.

"You'll wait at home this evening?"

"Right."

Minutes later, Gil called his friends who were preparing to sit in and be arrested in Congressman Fauntroy's office if that was necessary. Donna's news was encouraging for them, but not so much that their well-publicized demonstration would be aborted. They had sworn not to quit until some satisfactory agreement was actually reached. They had settled on several demands:

1. Assignment to a position in the line of march other than at the end.
2. Acceptance of a black gay speaker as a prominent part of the rally.
3. Endorsement of the National Gay Rights Bill by the National Coalition of Conscience.

Gilberto's job was to sit at home close to his telephone, waiting for it to ring. When four-thirty in the afternoon arrived, he knew his friends were entering Congressional offices and commencing their sit-in, because that was the plan. At six-thirty he knew the demonstrators had been arrested, because he saw it happen on the television news. Still his telephone was silent, mocking.

Gilberto paced his living room, nervously eating crackers and cheese as hours passed. He changed television channels frequently. After 9:00 P.M. the telephone rang on three separate occasions. Two of the calls were from gay acquaintances, one with impractical suggestions and the other complaining that the gay black community was making no progress because Gil was doing nothing. The third call was a wrong number.

Midnight found Gil twisting between hope and despair. Dialing the march's office, he found their lines busy. That was encouraging. At 12:30 A.M., Gilberto's telephone rang again.

"Hold on," said Donna, wearily. "We've got this all together now. Sorry it's so late."

Time no longer mattered. Gilberto listened patiently as the participants announced themselves. It was flattering to be part of that historic call.

Each person coming on the private network checked in by speaking his or her own name: The District of Columbia's nonvoting delegate to the United States Congress, "Reverend Walter Fauntroy"; the widow of Martin Luther King, Jr., "Coretta Scott King"; the executive director of the National Gay Task Force, "Virginia Apuzzo"; the president of the Southern Christian Leadership Conference, "Reverend Joseph Lowery"; the president of the National Organization for Women, "Judy Goldsmith"; the executive director of the National Association for the Advancement of Colored People, "Reverend Benjamin Hooks"; the executive director of the National Coalition of Black Gays, "Gilberto Gerald." And there were others.

Conversation began with reminiscences among the senior members of the Coalition of Conscience. Lowery, King, Hooks, and Fauntroy made it obvious that they held each other in great regard, and there was little doubt of their shared affection. Gerald—and Ginny Apuzzo, who had actually negotiated the call—were initially relegated to the status of outsiders who had become invited eavesdroppers.

"Hooks, Lowery, and King joked about past incidents in their life as activists," wrote Gilberto, "events I was not privy to. When it came time for me to speak, I tried very carefully to convey my indignation with the recent turn of events without being disrespectful. I felt it was ironic that I, a beneficiary of their struggles with racism in the 1950s and 60s, should be attempting to teach them something about oppression."

Gilberto also recalled, "It was difficult, explaining my feelings to Mrs. King and the others. It was painful, because I was talking to my shining heroes, trying to educate them about a subject I assumed they should already know. It was like being a small child, having to teach something to your parents.

"I spoke as a gay black person. I spoke of what it means to be oppressed, not only as a black person, but as a gay person. I said to the Coalition of Conscience that gay and lesbian blacks run the risk of being people without any community. I tried to explain what a terrible position we could be in if the gay community didn't want blacks, and the black community didn't want gays!"

Among the civil rights activists, Joseph Lowery seemed to be the individual most comfortable with gay rights. Mrs. King was deeply concerned about retaining the solidarity of their Coalition of Conscience. She felt very threatened about the possibility of the National Organization for Women, and the American Friends, and who knows how many others, pulling out of the march.

The easiest concession won was that the gay marchers would not be stuck at the end of the parade. Everyone conceded that a place in the middle was more suitable. More difficult was the question of having a gay or lesbian main speaker, visible for a full twenty minutes, to deliver a major address as would leaders of other national organizations. The march coalition stood fast in their resistance, maintaining that speaking time was already fully allocated. Their only allowance, which they would never better, was inclusion of a gay or lesbian speaker for three minutes as part of a group presentation called "Litany of Commitment."

The third gay demand was the most interesting. Reverend Lowery was careful to point out that inasmuch as

many unrepresented members of the Coalition of Conscience were ministers (who had preached hell and dam-
nation for homosexuals), he was certainly not empowered
to sign any National Gay Rights Bill on their behalf.

"Mrs. King spoke openly about the conservatism
among the black clergy," wrote Gilberto, "and expressed
concerns about whether or not the time was right to deal
with the lesbian and gay issue." Later, Gil recalled, "Mrs.
King was extremely concerned that the black community
was not prepared for this. But Ginny Apuzzo was ready
with the perfect rebuttal. She had committed to memory
excerpts from the letter Martin Luther King, Jr., had
written two decades earlier while a prisoner in the Birmingham jail."

"'Frankly, I have yet to engage in a direct-action campaign that was "well-timed" in view of those who have not
suffered unduly from the disease of segregation,'" Ginny
quoted, carefully enunciating King's words. "'For years
now I have heard the word "Wait!" It rings in the ear
of every Negro with piercing familiarity. This "Wait" has
almost always meant "Never." We must come to see, with
one of our distinguished jurists, that "justice delayed is
justice denied."'"

Martin Luther King, Jr.'s, ageless philosophy brought
back vivid memories. He had written, "There comes a
time when the cup of endurance runs over, and men are
no longer willing to be plunged into the abyss of despair.
I hope, sirs, you can understand our legitimate and un-
avoidable impatience."

"Amen," said somebody on the line.

The hour was late, but Ginny continued, recalling the
admonishment from another part of King's letter, which
read: "A tragic misconception of time is the strangely irrational notion that there is something in the very flow
of time that will inevitably cure all ills. Actually, time itself

is neutral; it can be used either destructively or constructively. More and more I feel that the people of ill will have used time much more effectively than have the people of good will. We will have to repent in this generation not merely for the hateful words and actions of the bad people, but for the appalling silence of the good people."

Somebody cleared his throat over the telephone. More than two hours had passed since the beginning of the conference call. Ginny Apuzzo glanced at a watch and hastened to conclude her powerful remembrance. "Human progress never rolls in on wheels of inevitability," the martyr had written. "It comes through the tireless efforts of men willing to be co-workers with God, and without this hard work, time itself becomes an ally of the forces of stagnation. We must use time creatively, in the knowledge that the time is always ripe to do right. Now is the time to make real the promise of democracy and transform our pending national elegy into a creative psalm of brotherhood. Now is the time to lift our national policy from the quicksand of racial injustice to the solid rock of human dignity."

When Ginny had finished quoting from selected passages, there were murmurs of approval. Apparently a new bond of unity had been forged. Members of the Coalition of Conscience held fast to the principle that they could not sign for the entire organization, but each individual agreed to publicly endorse the National Gay Civil Rights Bill. For some, including those arrested in Fauntroy's office, the compromise was less than what they wanted, and seemed like a defeat. It was, in fact, a great achievement.

The Mayor's Conference Room in the District of Columbia is fairly large. On Friday morning, August 26, 1983, it was jammed with reporters, and crowded with people of all colors from the gay community. Coaxial cables were strewn on the floor like writhing snakes, and a battery of television cameras lined the back wall.

Gilberto blinked away tears as he watched his heroes, Benjamin Hooks, Joseph Lowery, and all the others who had participated in the middle-of-the-night conference, make their way one after another into the room. Coretta Scott King arrived last. A hush came over the room as she entered.

Gilberto had never spoken to such a gathering. Standing behind a battery of microphones, he delivered his speech. "This is an historic occasion," he said. "Three important struggles are joined today: the women's movement, the civil rights struggle, and gay rights. I look forward to building on what is happening here. This is a new beginning."

Joseph Lowery said, "Twenty years ago we marched, and one year later, the 1964 Civil Rights Act was passed. It is now time to amend that act to extend its protections to lesbians and gay men."

A quarter of a million people marched in Washington, D.C., on Saturday, August 29, 1983, as a quarter of a million people had marched there in 1963. The main difference was that Martin Luther King, Jr., had become a vivid inspirational memory, and larger than life.

When King had spoken in front of the Lincoln Memorial, his was not the main speech. King had only been allotted several minutes to have his say—five treasured minutes that will last forever.

In 1983, writer and activist Audre Lorde, a charismatic, feminist black lesbian, stood not far from where Martin Luther King had stood. It was late in the hot afternoon, as it had been twenty years before when that other strong and powerful voice electrified the crowd.

"I am Audre Lorde," she said, "speaking for the National Coalition of Black Lesbians and Gay Men! Today's march openly joins the black civil rights movement and the gay civil rights movement in struggles we have always shared.

"We marched in 1963 with Dr. Martin Luther King, and we dared to dream that freedom would include us. Because not one of us is free to choose the terms of our living until all of us are free to choose.

"Today we march, lesbians and gay men, and our children, standing in our own names, together with all our struggling sisters and brothers here and around the world—in the Middle East, in Central America, in the Caribbean and Africa—sharing our commitment to work for a livable future.

"We know we do not have to become copies of each other in order to be able to work together. We know that when we join hands across the table of our difference, diversity gives us power. When we can arm ourselves with the strength and vision from our diverse communities, then we will in truth, all of us—be free at last!"

The Litany of Commitment ended, and there were cheers and great shouts from the multitude. Perhaps not everyone entirely understood what they had heard. As for Gilberto, emotion, combined with Audre's words, compelled him to tears.

Sister Jean and
the Lavender Dinosaur

Some institutions seem to have existed since the beginning of time, and whether we always agree with them or not is secondary to the feeling of stability we generally derive from their centuries of endurance. Thus, it was a disappointing theological shock on October 1, 1986, when the prefect of the Catholic Church in Rome, with the approval of Pope John Paul II, declared war on the worldwide gay and lesbian community.

Joseph Cardinal Ratzinger's announcement was in the form of a printed pamphlet referred to in its title as a *Letter to the Bishops of the Catholic Church on the Pastoral Care of Homosexual Persons*—a pamphlet in which misstatements of science and homophobic distortions of Scripture appear to have been intentional. The little publication demonstrates how Vatican policy has currently become sidetracked from its Holy Mission by an obsessive inclination to dictate what people of the world may and may not do in any and all matters sexual.

It is common knowledge too that Rome is clearly displeased with America and the Western countries who have been stepping out of line with liberal thinking. As far back as 1976, Roman Catholic bishops in the United States published a pastoral letter entitled *To Live in Christ* wherein the bishops wrote, without any equivocation, that homosexuals "should not suffer from prejudice . . . they have a right to respect, friendship, and justice. They should have an active role in the Christian community." However, the Vatican makes it clear with their intolerable hard line that they now consider it improper for anybody to be fighting for the civil rights of lesbians or gay men. No doubt remains that Catholic policymakers want homosexuals to jump back into the closets—and quickly.

This is not the first time that the high priests in Rome have strayed far from Scripture and been unapologetically wrong in fields wherein they have no medical or scientific expertise. The pastoral letter of October 1, 1986, comes from the same organization that for centuries vociferously demanded God-fearing people believe the earth is flat, insisted the sun moves around the earth instead of vice versa, and declared that anything to the contrary was heresy and would be punished.

Cardinal Ratzinger's letter is a sophisticated form of gay-bashing, simultaneously inciting and excusing acts of violence against homosexual persons. The callous nature of this infamous document is self-evident. Ratzinger writes: "When civil legislation is introduced to protect [homosexual] behavior . . . neither the Church nor society at large should be surprised when . . . irrational and violent reactions increase." What a dreadful statement!

That such prejudicial, crime-provoking ideas were approved by a Pope who knows intimately of oppression in his native Poland is sad and extremely disappointing.

Furthermore, it seems that the prefect "doth protest too much" (while invoking the Vatican's cloak of infallibility). He, like us, undoubtedly has extensive personal knowledge of a great many Roman Catholic clergy—at all levels—who are homosexual.

Gay priests in the United States who have made headlines by refusing to be silent about their beliefs are only the tip of the iceberg. Some of the Americans braving the wrath of Rome have stated after serious consideration that homosexuality is "a blessing" (Reverend William Dorn, Jr.), that it is time for intelligent priests to be "disobedient" (Reverend Alan Eddington), and that Catholic distinctions between being gay and acting gay are "absurd" (Reverend John McNeil).

Other Catholic priests, not necessarily gay, have also taken a stand. Archbishop Raymond Hunthausen was stripped of considerable authority for allowing Dignity (an organization of gay and lesbian Catholics) to celebrate Mass in Seattle's Catholic cathedral.

Father Charles E. Curran's theological classes at Catholic University were terminated because of his dissenting views on human sexuality, including the observation that "homosexual acts in the context of a loving relationship striving for permanency can, in a certain sense, be morally acceptable."

Reverend Laurence Connelly, a parish priest in Sugarland, Texas, stated much more emphatically, "I am just sick and tired of what is going on!" He added that the Vatican's position on homosexuality is "anti-Christ and anti-Gospel." But many thousands of other gay Roman Catholic priests, men who are often practicing homosexuals, remain anonymous or silent.

According to researchers, educators, and many observant priests themselves, a disproportionate number of homosexuals are drawn into religious life. Thus, of the fifty-seven thousand Catholic priests and monks in America, not fewer than 20 percent are homosexual. Estimates from Father John Yockey of Washington Theological Union indicate that the figure of 40 percent is probably more accurate—although the latter is a percentage Rome's spokesmen are prone to dispute, preferring to settle for something in the range of 10 to 20 percent. Nevertheless, the statistics indicate that there are a minimum of eleven thousand (but more likely a total in excess of twenty-two thousand) gay Catholic priests and monks in the United States alone. The greatest contribution they could make to humanity or to heaven would be a braver support of their uncloseted brothers and sisters under attack.

Emancipation of gay Catholic priests and lesbian nuns can only come from inside their own ranks, and a perceptible move in such a direction clearly exists. The bold, honest, and eventually unified accomplishments of an increasing number of courageous individuals will undo locks from the cages of some members of the clergy. This challenge to Vatican authority is what bureaucrats like Ratzinger fear and would prevent.

In the Catholic Church (which has been magnificently glorified by famous homosexuals, including Michelangelo, who painted the Sistine Chapel, and Leonardo da Vinci, who gave us *The Last Supper*), men have not been braver than women. Given a different historical role, the generally sheltered life of a nun has probably been more difficult than the priesthood with its privileges has been for men; yet, dedicated women remaining in the Church, and disappointed women who leave, have often surpassed the contributions of males in the struggle for minority rights.

*   *   *

Jean O'Leary is one of the women who left the Church. For nearly five years, an intense half-decade, she was a nun. "I was only two and a half years away from taking my final vows when I concluded that the Church is too often a way of keeping people under the thumb of authority. I personally observed stifling repression to be a reality during the years I lived in the convent.

"My first inklings of the truth came from older nuns who were doing a lot of talking. They knew the Church wasn't always in the right. They thought the Church should be less concerned with what we could not do, and more concerned about what we could. The ghettos needed our help more than ever, but allowing nuns to establish work in sometimes dangerous areas was a revolutionary idea. We had to struggle for permission to go where our best protection would probably be ourselves.

"The lives we led would be enriched if we could increase our assistance to the needy, yet authorities in the Church were exceedingly reluctant to agree. Since then, bishops, and cardinals, and the latest Pope have changed their minds on the subject. But can you believe God's thinking has changed in twenty years? Can you believe that what was wrong then is okay today?

"Of course not! It's as silly as what was once a firm doctrine, now finally discarded, that it was a sin to eat meat on Friday. Intelligent correction of those outdated concepts gives us hope for a just solution in our present controversy concerning homosexuality. Someday, Church leaders may be blessed with a greater understanding of the human condition. If that day ever comes, it will be the beginning of peace in the world, theology will be more concerned with spirituality, and Rome's anointed few will need to run fast in renewed pursuit of love and goodness."

*   *   *

Jean was born in New York State in 1948. A few years later, growing up as a tomboy in Ohio, she did most of the things boys do. She played with a gang of kids and became their leader. They happily built forts and shot down beehives. They had exciting snowball fights in winter. When summer came, they played games in her Cleveland neighborhood, and in every game Jean played, there was always a mild, but discernible, streak of rebellion.

When she was very young, Jean attended an all-girl Catholic grammar school, Our Lady of the Elms. Several coed years at St. Sebastian followed. Then, finally, there was Magnificat, a beautiful Catholic high school. During her Magnificat years, Jean held the record for the number of times a student was required to stay after school. Three times she was threatened with being expelled, but her infractions were really high-spirited pranks.

Both of Jean's parents were very religious, yet not overly dramatic about their faith. At home, the O'Learys were comfortable. There was never a problem with money. The children were taught the value of a dollar and how to save. Jean often sold greeting cards door-to-door, earning enough to pay for her own tuition at Magnificat.

"I think I was probably the least likely kid to be ignored in the entire school," she recalls with a grin. "I was the class cutup. I considered running for office, but the school principal was afraid I might win and wouldn't allow my name on the ballot—knowing my potential for creative disruption.

"So I nominated my best friend for the same office, and I soon learned that running her campaign was just as much fun as running myself. It was a great experience. We had posters everywhere. I had musical bands trumpeting through the cafeteria at lunchtime! And everyday I dreamed up something different.

"But wait—

"Do you know what that expended energy was? It was me striving to attract attention—wanting to be close with the people I cared for! But never actually having sex with anybody, yet. Not that I didn't want to! I wanted love, but I had no desire to do anything which would cause me to become an outcast. I wasn't ready to ignore social sanctions. The rest of my life might be in the balance if I made a mistake. Of only one thing was I definitely certain—that I wanted to love and be loved by women."

Sister Mary Patrick and Sister Mary Joseph were the recipients of Jean's esteem in Jean's junior year. She thought Sister Mary Patrick was the most intelligent woman on the school staff and admired her with a special love. Partly for herself, and partly to impress Sister Mary Patrick, Jean began reading philosophy and ethics, devouring books by theologians. Meanwhile, Sister Joseph was more accessible. Sister Joseph, always an inspirational friend, enjoyed the playful manifestations of Jean's initiatives and patiently tried to steer her adventurous vitality into paths of acceptable behavior. As a result, without using pressure, the teacher was responsible for Jean's decision to enter a convent.

"I went to a retreat," said Jean, "and when I came back after two weeks, I had weighed a number of factors and decided to become a nun. The idea was not a stranger, having been in my mind for some time, although the final decision was arrived at very quickly. I was following instincts that have always served me well, and I would like to stress, no matter what extraneous feelings I may have had, I was devoutly sincere and believed in everything I said and did. I truly felt that I had a calling from God.

"But people were shocked!

"Some of my friends felt betrayed. What do you say to the bad person who turns ultragood? It was like in the movie *The Trouble with Angels*. My schoolgirl companions no longer wanted to confide in me about their affairs with boys, about being afraid of getting pregnant—things that I, naturally, would never think of doing!

"I was chosen to give the senior class speech in the main auditorium before an assembly of our entire school. It was the first public speech of my life; and realizing the honor that had been bestowed upon me, I carefully wrote the words well in advance and carefully rehearsed. The speech was entitled 'What Magnificat Means to Me,' and the text was from my heart. When I stood in front of everybody, my nervousness evaporated. It was all wonderfully dramatic—including the announcement that I was going into a convent—and why I was embracing the ultimate marriage of faith. I felt it was the higher calling we should all set our sights on. I was becoming a nun for the glory of God!"

There was a standing ovation from all the classes and the faculty, including Sister Mary Joseph and Sister Mary Patrick. Even Jean herself was moved. And Mr. and Mrs. O'Leary were very proud.

Postulants entering a convent study to be nuns. Everything else is superfluous. In their future, whenever and however called to serve, they are expected to respond. Usually some choices exist, but there are occasions when sisters submit quietly to a Heavenly Will as interpreted by the church's earthly authority.

Four and a half years in a convent had more to do with the shaping of Jean's life than anything that had happened to her before. The teaching-nursing order to which she belonged was relatively liberal despite restrictions; and because what has come to be known as Vatican II was happening, there were attempts to try new ideas within the confines of the convent. During Sister Jean's second year, sensitivity groups that encouraged the cloistered young women to plunge into psychological self-examination were held weekly; and in that closely knit assemblage where emotions reverberated continuously, there developed such perilously intense reactions that only people with considerable ego-strength emerged unscathed. Several novices returned home before the project was abandoned. Two attempted suicide. Neither was successful.

As for Jean, she instinctively knew that the emotional explorations were having a more valuable impact upon her than any other lessons. "It was an incredible experience in a confined environment," she said. "I constantly stayed up until four or five o'clock every morning, exploring my own feelings, learning who I was and learning what the games are that people play, bluntly coming to grips with my strengths and weaknesses, and defining my defenses." It was a large step toward maturity.

At the same time, Sister Jean made a concerted effort to discover a greater appreciation of something more intangible within herself. She would often kneel in the convent's serene, inviting chapel and pray, trying all the steps of meditation with great conviction. Striving for pure thoughts in those peaceful, spiritually conducive surroundings, Jean felt close to experiencing a communion of God and soul.

"When I went into the convent, I thought I was going in because I had a calling," she recalls. "In retrospect, I know it was because I was a lesbian and wanted to be with women. When I was growing up, I'd had a recurring fantasy about living on an island populated with females,

and there were no men around. I believe that's why, un-
consciously, I chose to be a nun.

"I don't think a large percentage of nuns are lesbians.
Women go into the convent for many reasons. To begin,
a great many nuns are totally sincere, and that should be
emphasized. Then there is another group, women with
different kinds of problems. Some problems are in the
sexual arena: frigidity, fear of men, et cetera. And there
is a vivid spectrum of behavior involving obedience. Some
people simply have an overwhelming need to be told
what to do. As for vows of poverty, I doubt if they're
truly an attraction—I haven't found anybody yet who's
sincerely interested in being poor!

"To become a full-fledged nun takes about seven years.
I was well on my way toward reaching final vows when I decided to leave. Generally, the departure process is long and
involved. You are encouraged to agonize over the decision.
However, what I agonized about was being sexual.

"When you enter the convent, you take a vow of chastity.
I found that was a problem when I wanted to explore my
emotions with other women. As a result, I was often trying
to rationalize by redefining our vow as being one of "holy
chastity" instead of "physical chastity," an idea which
found absolutely no academic support. In Chastity class,
vindication would not be provided with semantics.

"At night I would stand by a tall, thin window at the
end of the hall and stare out at the night, not caring if
the weather was rainy or windy or cold, but just saying
to myself, 'God, I have to face up to it. There really is
something different about me. My being in this convent
is nothing more than an escape. I can't stay here being
the way I am. I'll have to leave.' And then, sometimes,
almost on cue as I remember, clouds sweeping across the
sky would pass in front of the moon and I'd be standing

in darkness at the end of that long corridor, alone, dismayed because everything seemed so terribly wrong.

"But the next morning, when the sun came up and its brightness flooded my room, I would feel like a different person, and would try to brush aside doubts. After all, I didn't want to leave. I loved that place! The nunnery was a special island.

"My feelings of attachment had a lot to do with the convent being a female environment, and there was the subtle, pervasive thrill of actually making love. When I embraced another woman, it would be in the recreation room or behind a hanging sheet. We had only a minimum of privacy, and there was always the considerable danger of being observed. On the plus side, there was no pressure to go with a boy to a prom, and no expectation or worry about getting married.

"The convent was my emotional heaven. I enjoyed the company of novice friends, and others, including our postulant mistress. But when the uncertain hours of night returned, sleep was banished by some inner urge. I was frequently reminded that a different way of life was calling!"

Jean chafed against life as a nun for several reasons. One was a frustrating conflict she faced during her novitiate years. Following undergraduate work at Youngstown University, she was earning an approved Bachelor of Arts degree at Cleveland State University where, like most students, she became unhappy about the war in Vietnam. When a national peace gathering was organized to march on Washington, Sister Jean hoped to be a part of the protest.

"But Sister, why do you think you should attend such a rally?" queried the mother superior, who was petitioned for permission.

"Because I believe it's something important," Jean patiently tried to explain.

"But, Sister, don't you have a more explicit reason?"

"Well, I feel the war is wrong," said Jean, "and I want to be involved in what's happening. After all, if not peace and love, what's religion all about?"

Jean's petition was denied.

"I began to realize, firsthand, that the religious hierarchy was not precisely correct on all occasions. Among my peers in the convent there was a lot of questioning going on about what women's roles in the church could be, and really should be. And there were major doubts as to how much of our doctrine legitimately came from On High, and how much was the result of secular, institutionalized power."

Another disappointment for Sister Jean was that, one way or another, all her closest friends, particularly those in the class ahead of her own, were leaving. Jean felt as if her heart was breaking. A lifetime of involuntary separations is something nuns accept. For Jean, the idea became too painful.

Her resolution to leave the convent matured over a period of about a year, and when she had finally put all the reasons for staying and all the reasons for leaving on the scale, the latter outweighed the former, and a firm decision to leave was made. Characteristically, Jean rejected the idea of spending months in contemplation. Within a fortnight, her bags were packed and she made the rounds saying good-bye to everyone, particularly a few special friends who still remained. A sister's abrupt departure can be very traumatic, even devastating for some who stay behind. With that knowledge, Jean made every effort to leave each woman with whatever reassurances were necessary, and she gave different reasons for her departure.

She told only three people that she was leaving because she was a homosexual. Another story was given to everyone else. Jean herself was still having difficulty accepting the truth—but two years later, she would be the world's most outspoken lesbian!

In 1970, at twenty-one years of age, and still relatively innocent, Jean O'Leary was anxious to face the world. She moved to Greenwich Village "intending to find the lesbians," and she temporarily shared a small studio apartment with a man who had been a dean at Cleveland State University. He was gay. She was a lesbian. But neither knew about the other for weeks. When they went out together, they went only to heterosexual places.

For a brief period, Jean continued going to church. Then she stopped. Religion, which had been the primary part of Jean's life, was now substantially behind her. "I figuratively put it in a box and floated it down the Hudson River," she said. "I'm sure my reactions were because of the Church's unrelenting attitude on homosexuality, telling me that I was bad, a sinner, and damned to hell. With the brain God gave me, I instinctively knew better!"

Nearly a month after Jean's arrival in New York, her roommate went out of the city for the weekend. On that Friday evening, looking for something to do, Jean decided to examine a book that she had seen him place high in his bookcase, laying it flat, nearly out of sight on the top of other volumes. An unintentional flash of its title had revealed two words that demanded Jean's attention. The words were *gay* and *militant*.

She stood on a low stool, and rising on tiptoe, reached for the book. As she grasped its binding, Jean's foot slipped. She fell, clutching the cover, while papers that had been placed between pages landed on the hardwood floor. No damage was done, and to Jean's delight, scattered around her was all kinds of information about gay and lesbian activities. That night she found a bar that was advertised.

It was one of the tough lesbian "role" bars. They were "the only games in town" for women in those years. Customers, almost exclusively female, were expected to act either "butch" or "femme," and looked the same. Thirty minutes elapsed before Jean gathered sufficient courage to quit walking back and forth on the block outside of the establishment, and enter. Much to her surprise, with the exception of a couple of bartenders, the premises were nearly empty. But the hour was early. Patrons would soon arrive.

Jean ordered beer, and while she waited in the stale, as yet unfamiliar surroundings, she asked many questions. Until this point, Jean had never felt that she fully knew what she was doing with her own life. But arriving in New York was like "coming home."

She quickly began making friends with other lesbians.

"I could hardly believe it!" Jean said. "I went on a date, and suddenly realized I was out. I was finally doing something real in society, instead of under false pretenses like in high school. It wasn't a convent fantasy. I was being myself. I was filled with euphoria, ecstatic!

"There was no question in my mind about what I was going to do next. I was going to jump right into the gay movement with both feet—and damn the consequences! It was the happy time! It was great!"

In 1970, when Jean began her activist career, the gay movement was composed almost entirely of men. Only three members of the Gay Activists Alliance were women when Jean joined, and the female trio had the questionable distinction of being designated as the "Subcommittee of the Human Relations Committee of the Gay Activists

Alliance." If the length of that title was not in itself sufficient cause for the women to break away from the men,
Jean recalls that "overt and constant sexism was."

The split occurred a year and six months after Jean
joined the Alliance, when she and a growing number of
other women, tired of being surrogate mothers and sisters, decided it was time to move ahead on their own.
With little support and minimal funds, they gathered
their courage and formed the first lesbian civil rights
group in America—Lesbian Feminist Liberation. It still
exists today, and it is the largest organization of its kind
in the State of New York.

Before the Stonewall Rebellion in Greenwich Village in
1969, and before the founding of Metropolitan Community Church in Los Angeles the previous year, when gay
and lesbian cooperation was in its infancy, the largest
group of out-of-the-closet individuals, as often as not,
were nonapologetic people who attempted to imperson-
ate the opposite sex. Transvestites, with whom a large
percentage of homosexuals could not identify, were unquestionably the vanguard of gay liberation. They were
the First Generation of gays to be highly visible, and the
first to defend their rights in a time when few others had
found the courage to be identified.

Nearly concurrent with Stonewall, however, several
new groups came into existence—with New York's radical
Gay Activists Alliance in the forefront. These groups
were part of the Second Generation in a modern history
of the homosexual's uphill battle against oppression.
Knowing gay men and lesbians were ill-treated and without redress, they were convinced that nothing could ever
be accomplished until people everywhere—including millions of homosexuals themselves, and potential friends
and potential foes alike—became aware not only of griev-

ances, but also of the tens of millions of silent gay people who had no knowledge of each other's existence.

Much of what the Gay Activists Alliance and Lesbian Feminist Liberation did, therefore, usually had one primary objective: to break a universal media blackout. That meant they wanted to be seen on television (which was nearly impossible); wanted to be mentioned on the radio (which was also nearly impossible); wanted to get people talking no matter what they would say; wanted to get the word to millions of homosexuals that they had brothers and sisters who were beginning to fight against traditional persecution; and wanted to tell the world, whether the world wanted to hear it or not, that homosexuals do—and will—continue to exist.

It didn't matter that the few terse references media chose to make concerning homosexuals were usually homophobic as well as inaccurate. Vile recognition was better than nothing at all. The early activists all knew that issues could not be confronted until they were widely verbalized. "The love that dare not speak its name" had, indeed, been silent for centuries, and that needed to be changed before there could be any progress.

Treating 10 percent of the population as though they did not exist was the real oppression; and the most powerful tool in the battle against invisibility—used frequently in the days following Stonewall—was called "the zap"! Zaps consisted of imaginative and surprising actions—like handcuffing slogan-chanting members to fixtures where televised formal banquets were in progress, or throwing radical, progay literature over balconies into the midst of unsuspecting concert-goers. Anything for a single word in the press or a blurred picture on television!

"We were reacting from the ugliest oppression anyone could ever imagine," said Jean. "Everybody treated us like dirt, like we were beneath contempt! Yet our reactions were not always ugly, but could, on occasion, have a charm reflecting our inner sensibilities."

New York's Museum of Natural History had many exhibits that some members of Lesbian Feminist Liberation concluded were sexist, homophobic, or both, and the women decided the museum should have its consciousness raised. With the primary idea of attracting attention, they attempted to make an issue by asking the curators to reconsider their displays. For instance, Lesbian Feminist Liberation felt a good step would be for the museum to stop referring to exhibits as scenes of prehistoric "man" and begin calling them scenes of prehistoric "people." Although the dictionary defines man as meaning both male and female persons in certain contexts, actual usage, they argued, had too often ignored women or relegated women to an inferior position. With this and similar revisions in mind, a position paper of well over a hundred scholarly pages was developed; but the treatise was written in vain, having zero impact on conservative museum officials.

"It quickly became obvious that we were not ready to exert influence upon one of the most staid institutions in New York," Jean admits. "Nevertheless, we were not ready to quit.

"On a concrete pad behind the apartment building where one of our members lived, we assembled old wooden planks, wheels, chicken wire, paint, newspapers, paste, and many other items. We worked steadily, laughing and grouching over a period of four weeks, until we were able to put together a big, amateurish thing the likes of which the world had surely never seen before, a lavender dinosaur made of papier-mâché. Our muscle power and determination would be its twin sources of propulsion.

"The dinosaur was twenty feet long, and its grinning head was fourteen feet high, more than large enough to slow traffic around us as we moved the colorful creature down Broadway. We didn't lack for attention, in the center of Manhattan, during the busiest hours of the day! Media were there to take pictures because we had called them in advance, and attracted their curiosity. When pictures were taken and we had accomplished what was intended, all of us were worn out from dragging the inanimate lavender beast through the crowded streets. That was the moment a disapproving policeman chose to begin demanding information about what we were going to do with our huge creation.

"'You can have it, officer,' I told him. But one of our members wanted the dinosaur for a souvenir, and we dragged it home with us.

"The Gay Activists Alliance was formed almost immediately following the Stonewall Rebellion, with the specific intention that we should have a gay civil rights bill passed into law for the boroughs of New York City. Very righteously, we set out to get it. 'Gay rights! Gay rights!' all of us exclaimed, but not many were listening.

"So we combed the boroughs and got enough signatures on a petition to bring our bill before the City Council, where it failed, not once, but on an annual basis. Determined, we returned with our proposal year after year for a very long time until it finally passed, but the struggle was really terrible.

"Our document was best known as Intro 475, and it was always opposed by the same organized groups. The worst verbal dissent came from the New York Fire Department, the New York Police, and Hasidic Jews. Their vicious, dehumanizing antagonism was a vile combination of self-righteousness and stupidity that was repeated at public hearings held year after year.

"The testimony would be structured to allow one of our opponents to speak against the gay rights bill and then one of us to speak for it, alternating; and we had to sit in churchlike pews across the aisle from our adversaries, while they used their turns at speaking to call us every filthy name in the book. It became so low! A terrible, scraggly man insisted we were 'unpure, unholy dogfuckers!' That was in the large courtroom in New York's City Hall. He and his friends were so evil, or so bigoted, or both, that I would often get close to tears.

"During the hearings, partisan applause was deafening. The shouts were deafening. Insults were deafening. For a couple of years we had transvestites and transsexuals, and other radical fringe groups, engaging in major demonstrations in the back of the hearing room or up in the balcony. Members of the City Council would be banging their gavels and shouting, 'I'm going to bring these hearings to a close if we can't have some order here!' But there was little order. It was a zoo. We didn't want it to be a zoo, but the media loved it. All of us took part in demonstrations every time we lost. Passion ran high on both sides.

"In the beginning, fury was the only thing we had, but eventually, we got smarter and discovered how New York is controlled. We began to talk to the real bosses, men who pull the strings. Unfortunately, at that time we were still a poor, and thus powerless, lobby (the capability of raising money for politicians is what holds their attention). We had learned, however, that people in public life don't like being demonstrated against. As a result, zapping continued to be the most powerful ace in the hole for the Gay Activists Alliance and our Lesbian Feminist Liberation."

*   *   *

When the time arrived that the word "homosexuality" could be mentioned in public, albeit nervously, the radicals had done their work. Individuals then followed who wanted the gay movement to begin moving its way up the political ladder. Unhappy with the Gay Activists Alliance's constant internal bickering for nonexistent power, they began forming a Third Generation of community organizations.

In 1974, Dr. Bruce Voeller, with his extensive academic and literary credentials, together with a few other people, founded the National Gay Task Force—which exists today as the National Gay and Lesbian Task Force. Bruce had been a president of the Gay Activists Alliance, and before coming out as a gay person, had been married and was the father of several children.

Shortly after the Task Force was founded, Jean contacted Bruce to explore the possibility of becoming part of the new group. She, like its other members, felt she had outgrown the difficult, grass-roots years; and when Bruce realized that Jean was not as radical as her Lesbian Feminist Liberation activities had led outsiders to believe, and when it became obvious that Jean had much to contribute to a different, more mainstream type of activity, she was asked to join. Not many months later, Jean's energy, imagination, and continuing contributions earned her a leadership position as the coexecutive director of the National Gay Task Force.

Yet some problems were no different from what they had been previously. It was still not easy to obtain any attention for national gay rights issues. There was a continuing need for the Task Force to impress upon the media that an important cultural movement was taking place, and that its participants should not be scoffed at or degraded as "some bunch of queers or faggots doing their thing"!

Ron Gold and Ginny Vida were Jean's media directors. Together they mounted a major effort for any and all kinds of national television exposure. For a long time the objective seemed impossible to achieve. It was as if homosexuals did not exist, even though it was clear to those aware of existing scientific research that there were many millions of middle-class homosexuals in every job and every imaginable walk of life.

A major breakthrough occurred when NBC television aired a segment in which Jean participated on "The Today Show" and spoke of homosexual issues. Articles in several major magazines followed. The result was electric in the lesbian and gay community. The "love that dare not speak it's name" had spoken. The closet door was inching open. It would not be closed again. Nevermore! *It's Time!* was the name of the Task Force's newsletter. The name was prophetic.

Until this period, it had been common practice for doctors to methodically label homosexuals as being a sick body of people—a terrible error of fact, however hoary the use of such terminology. So, to counteract the sickness myth (which every new study was proving unfounded), the National Gay Task Force directed much of its energy toward lobbying members of the American Psychiatric Association to review their thinking. Highly motivated by Dr. Voeller, the Task Force conducted a lengthy, multitiered educational program until a majority of American psychiatrists officially joined in agreement and voted to abolish the prejudicially inaccurate "sickness" theory.

"We had been riding the coattails of peace and other civil rights movements that began in the sixties," said

Jean, "but in 1974, I remember taking a deep breath and saying to myself, 'We've made it—homosexuals are an acceptable civil rights issue now!' With gay rights becoming a bona fide social topic, it finally became possible for educated heterosexual people to come out in support of our position. After some well-known academic, medical, and psychiatric personalities had made that leap, others began to follow without the fear of being labeled gay or lesbian (which seemed to be about the worst thing you could be labeled at the time)."

Of the important lessons Jean O'Leary has learned, one is that when you require something, you go get it; another is, when you need a new organization, you create it. That initiative has served Jean and the gay and lesbian community well. Working from within the established democratic system, Jean's social and political accomplishments on a national level have been extensive. The tomboy who shot down beehives has traveled a difficult road, using obstacles that might defeat others for stepping-stones to achievement.

At the 1976 Democratic National Convention in New York, Jean was an elected delegate, thus becoming the first openly gay person, male or female, ever to vote in such an assembly. During Carter's Administration, Jean was appointed to the President's National Commission on the Observance of International Women's Year, where, after considerable work, she was successful in having "Sexual Orientation" included on the national feminist agenda (which had never considered the subject before). Later, in 1980, at the next National Democratic Convention, which was held in San Francisco, Jean was a special delegate appointed by Senator Ted Kennedy.

O'Leary has also been a founder and served on the

boards of directors of numerous national gay, feminist, and political organizations. In 1981, Jean became the executive director of National Gay Rights Advocates, a nearly defunct public-interest law firm, and made it into one of the largest gay and lesbian organizations existing today in the field of civil rights. N.G.R.A. promotes gay equality, and is a resource for information concerning related issues.

A project that Jean particularly likes to recall involved the White House. After Jimmy Carter took office in 1976, Jean contacted Midge Costanza (the first female senior staff assistant to any President of the United States). Jean and Midge had previously aided each other pushing platform initiatives within the Democratic Party. They were friends, and Jean was close enough to ask a favor.

When Costanza answered the White House telephone in her office next to the President's, Jean was on the line. "Midge," she said, "I think it's time gay people stopped picketing the White House on the outside. I think it's time to ask for a meeting on the inside! What do you say?"

There is a possibility that Midge choked on the other end of the telephone line. Trying not to sound overly surprised, she said, "Is that all you want?"

"It will be historic! And it will be effective!" answered Jean enthusiastically, adding, "Besides, it goes right along with the President's 'human rights' ideas."

A pause followed. Midge apparently was making some difficult decisions. When she replied, she said, "You set up the meeting, and I'll make arrangements to have it here."

"Wonderful!" exclaimed Jean, becoming excited. She was mentally working on the project even before she put down the telephone. Twelve gay and lesbian leaders from around the country would be picked to attend, plus Bruce Voeller and herself. Each would be asked to present position papers on different homosexual matters.

Months later, on March 26, 1977, the gay and lesbian meeting took place within the White House as scheduled. Midge Costanza, White House personnel, and civil rights specialists were the hosts. In addition to Dr. Voeller and Jean O'Leary, invited guests were Massachusetts state legislator Elaine Noble; Washington, D.C., activist Dr. Franklin Kameny; founder of Metropolitan Community Church, Reverend Troy Perry; editor of the feminist quarterly *Quest*, Charlotte Bunch; lesbian-activist Pokey Anderson from Houston; president of Seattle's Dorian Society, Charles Brydon; Cookie Lutkefedder; Mary Mendola; Brooklyn College instructor Betty Powell; San Francisco lobbyist George Raya; psychiatric therapist Myra Riddell; and the founder of Parents and Friends of Gays in Los Angeles, Charlotte Spitzer.

During a break, members of the press and television corps asked questions of the delegates. "Does President Carter know this meeting is going on?" asked a correspondent from CBS.

"Yes, he does," was the official White House reply.

Presidential Press Secretary Jody Powell added for the benefit of reporters, "I think that when an organized group of people feel they are not being treated fairly in this country we live in, it is their right to put their grievance before the officials of the land and say, 'We want redress.' That is what America is all about."

In the next couple of years, results of those presentations were felt in numerous areas of federal influence, including the State Department, Immigration and Naturalization, Civil Service, Housing and Urban Development, the Justice Department, the U.S. Civil Rights

Commission, and the Federal Bureau of Prisons. All were governmental bodies that had been dealing badly with homosexuals, and their top leaders generally agreed to become more reasonable in dealing with gay and lesbian people simply because the President of the United States wanted it to happen.

Women, blacks, veterans, et cetera, had long been recognized by the Federal Communications Commission as legitimate minority groups. The FCC utilized watchdog organizations to monitor the media so those minorities would receive fair portions of broadcast coverage. Homosexuals had never been included as a viable group, and—with a few memorable exceptions—received almost no broadcast reporting at all. But that changed as a direct result of the White House meeting. Homosexuals became a legitimate minority group. It was a major achievement.

"But I hate to see two years of incredibly hard work summed up in two paragraphs," said Jean. "Working through bureaucratic red tape, grinding out agreements behind the scenes in an endless series of meetings, was total drudgery. Even with the President's sanction, there was tremendous opposition. We were attempting to wear out our opponents, and for a time there was incredible progress—although some of it did not last forever. During the Carter Administration, advances were in the form of policy from the President or others near the top. Executive Orders are not law, however; and with Ronald Reagan's election to the presidency, a number of ideas and feelings about minorities reverted back to what they had been before Jimmy Carter's term in office. That leads to the essence of what I think our whole movement is about.

"We work on issues, trying to have a meaningful impact wherever we can, trying to make some lasting changes. We still need zaps to maintain public attention even though all sectors of the population, including whites, blacks, and blue-collar workers come into speaking contact with us every day. Lesbians and gay men are achievers within the ranks of any sizable organization you can name, and knowingly or otherwise, everybody talks with us. The bottom line is that we are positioned everyplace in society—we are everywhere!

"Our focus on the media today is a little different from what it was a few years ago. Now, responsible media personalities usually say positive things about us, even though we have to convince some reporters who are still too prejudiced to check out the truth.

"I am strongly in favor of whatever upgrades public attitudes and enhances our reputation. We are making enormous strides toward acceptability. We are not trying to get there, we are there. We're trying to stay put when people find out we're gay. That's why our slogan has never been 'gay jobs.' It is always 'Gay Pride'!"

There was a time when some feminists told Jean that she should not work in what most often are predominantly male organizations. But as past president of the National Association of Business Councils and later executive director of National Gay Rights Advocates, Jean's response was, "Are you kidding? I set the agenda!"

"I think our people are coming to realize there are no 'men's issues' or 'woman's issues'—that we rise and fall together," Jean O'Leary says. "Where women have strengths, we should use them. Where men have strengths, we should use them. That's what will make our movement powerful. I really do believe, for the first time, that there is a sincere recognition of the happiness to be achieved working together. We've seen it in little pockets here and there. I've enjoyed it all my life. Seeing thousands of homosexual men and women working together is very encouraging!"

75 CENTS

SEPTEMBER

TIME

"I Am a Homosexual"

The Gay Drive for Acceptance

MATLOVICH

American
Eagle

vvvvvvvvvvvvvvvvvvvvvvvvvvvvvvvvvvvvvvvvvvvvvvvvvvvvvvvvvvvvvvvvvv

Lieutenant (j.g.) Dan Miller, age twenty-four, after two weeks of solitary confinement in the brig at Subic Bay, Philippine Islands, was transferred to Fort Leavenworth in Kansas, location of the American Armed Forces' high-security prison—there to complete his sentence of a year at hard labor in the company of other military felons, traitors, rapists, murderers, etc. Dan Miller's crime? In his private, sixth-floor apartment off the base in Guam, Miller engaged in casual homosexual activity with two consenting adults, gay sailors who had served with him (but not under his command) on a supply vessel based at the island. Naval Intelligence, while engaged in other investigations, had stumbled upon information concerning Miller's sexual orientation, and in exchange for sworn testimony condemning the officer, gave immunity to the sailors involved. As a result, Miller was sentenced to twelve months of hard labor and stripped of his pay and benefits.

The story sounds like something that might have been

recorded a hundred years ago. Actually, it happened in what is sometimes referred to as the "modern" United States Navy.

"I was appalled," said Sergeant Jim Highland, a U.S. Army veteran from World War II, founder of the Veterans' Council for American Rights and Equality (representing a conservative estimate of four million gay veterans from all services, including the U.S. Coast Guard). "There are people in high places in the military who are functionally illiterate on the subject of sex. Their thinking is inbred in those self-perpetuating military academies, and they only know what they tell each other, which is barbarically wrong from the start. Frankly, I'm surprised they forgot to have Lieutenant Miller walk the plank! The United States Navy is one of those primal type organizations that continue to insist that all gay people are sick."

Miller's sentence was pronounced on November 13, 1985, by military judge Captain Peter H. Strow. What prejudicial background experience clouded his judgment we can only guess. When asked for a comment, Strow declined. However, *The Los Angeles Times* quoted a Navy commander from San Diego, who said, "I don't know of anyone going to jail for homosexuality. I don't know how they're going to come up with an explanation. There's no rhyme or reason to it!"

Fortunately for Dan Miller, Rear Admiral Edwin R. Kahn, Jr., under pressure from various sources, including Miller's dauntless mother, reduced the sentence to two months, and Dan was released from Leavenworth. The resolution is not happy, however, because in Dan's own words, "The fact remains, the Navy prosecuted me, and I will be considered a convicted felon."

As a civilian, Miller would have received similar treatment in five states of the Union. According to *Newsweek* in July 1986, Alabama, Arkansas, Kentucky, Minnesota, and Missouri prescribed a maximum jail sentence of up to one full year for homosexual sodomy. In 1986, some other states were (and many continue to be) considerably more harsh. On the books in Idaho, Louisiana, Nevada, South Carolina, and Virginia were five-year and six-year sentences. In Maryland, Mississippi, Montana, North Carolina, Oklahoma, and the District of Columbia the sentence was ten years. Michigan, strangely selective, handed out five years for oral sex and fifteen years for anal. Tennessee wanted fifteen years either way. And the worst sentences in the United States were in Georgia and Rhode Island—twenty years—a much worse sentence than murderers receive in many American courts today.

In Arizona, Florida, Kansas, and Utah, time in jail ranged from thirty days to six months for homosexual sodomy. (Heterosexual sodomy was *not* unlawful in five of the states with sodomy laws.) Texas charged a fine of two hundred dollars—for gays only!

Twenty-six states, particularly those in the Northeast and on the Pacific Coast, have rewritten what were antiquated laws and have now decriminalized sodomy. These enlightened advancements commenced in 1961 with the sporadic realization that in a free country the nature of sexual activities engaged in by consenting adults in private is not the business of the government, any group, or individual. In 1986, the Gallup Organization discovered that 75 percent of Americans polled believed states have no right to regulate what goes on privately in heterosexual bedrooms; 57 percent (definitely a comedown, but still a viable majority) believed that homosexual persons should have rights equal to those of heterosexuals.

Therefore, it becomes encouragingly obvious that there is a very real trend toward tolerance in the United States. No such statement can be made for the United States Armed Forces. Policies that were formulated well before the Civil War remain the same today—not because the policies were ever wise or venerable but because the military mind often is not. Too few of our leaders in the Armed Forces of America, despite their prowess in war, have the mental dexterity to free themselves of sexual prejudice that works to the disservice of the homosexual community, and is a disservice to the military itself. The story of Technical Sergeant Leonard Matlovich is a case in point.

"When I was about four, my father, an Air Force noncommissioned officer was stationed on Guam. As we approached the island, our ship picked its way past Pacific atolls where the remains of wrecked World War II Japanese landing craft were rusting in the clear, shallow waters. I began to have fantasies of the recent war and, in my childish daydreams, imagined that wounded Marines were on the coral sands, waiting for my assistance. I wanted to get off the ship to help and to hold them.

"As I grew older, living where my father was stationed—Pennsylvania, Alaska, South Carolina, and England—I came to envision myself in the medical field. If I were a corpsman, I could touch men—not sexually, but to comfort, caress, and make them better. I didn't know I was homosexual. As things worked out, while living in England, I joined the United States Air Force at the age of eighteen. Because of a written aptitude test, the powers that be made me an electrician instead of a medic."

Leonard had no construction skills and knew nothing about electricity. "I didn't even know what a screwdriver was before I joined the Air Force," grinned Matlovich, "but I became a very good electrician. I was proud of the work I did."

Training was an enjoyable period—living with men, acquiring knowledge, and mastering fears. In the latter category, Leonard had always had an inordinate dislike for heights; but in the military, when it was time to practice clambering up forty-five-foot-high telephone poles, there was no permission not to climb. As a result, Leonard went up the tall poles again and again, until he went beyond being confident. He became cocky!

"At the end of the week, we were to learn how to climb to the top without a safety belt," he said. "I had been doing so well, and began showing off. I was way up the pole when—shwaap!—the gaff came out! Down I went! Everything blurred, and there was little time to think. When I hit the ground, I landed outstretched, flat on my back. Considering the distance I fell, I should have been killed. There is no explanation of how I escaped injury. I wasn't even knocked out.

"I knew that if I didn't go back up that pole right then and there, I would never climb again. My feet were shaking, but I went all the way to the top without a belt, and came back down again. After that I was okay. I was ready to climb whenever necessary."

But when training was over, Matlovich's duties never required any work on poles. He was sent to Vietnam where he had an opportunity to do something he had long wanted—to prove himself. He would prove his "manhood," he figured, or die in the attempt. "This is an awful thing to admit," Matlovich said, "but it shows what being in the closet can do to the mind. I had always been worried that there would *not* be a war in which I could fight. I wanted to be in combat! Isn't that sick? I so desperately wanted to prove myself. I was continually trying to prove I was as brave or as good as any other man around. If I was maybe a 'queer,' or a 'faggot,' or a 'fairy' inside (being celibate, I didn't know for certain), I still wanted to prove I wasn't afraid to go fight and die for my country!"

During his first tour in Nam, Matlovich and a hundred and fifty other airmen were placed at an isolated radar site close to the demilitarized zone. Leonard was the electrician. "With our radar," he said, "we directed American bombers that were going into North Vietnam. If there was cloud cover, we would give them their location. If planes were shot down, we could direct rescue helicopters that were sent to find them.

"We were frequently under attack. Under those circumstances, I would crawl out alone to the other side of the perimeter. There I would set up lights so our machine gunners could see to shoot whoever was shooting at us. Crawling around in a minefield, dragging rugged electrical cables to hook up generator-powered spotlights, was not easy. There were close calls—being sprayed by gunfire from a short distance. That went on for over a year. Eventually, I got our lights set up more or less permanently. Then all we had to do was throw a switch, and the area was illuminated. It was my idea to see whom we were shooting. And there was hope our lights would blind the enemy from seeing us."

Leonard and Father Valour, a French priest, became good friends. (Matlovich's father was Polish; his mother was Irish—it almost goes without saying that Leonard was born Catholic.) When Leonard went to confession, the only "sin" he had to worry about was masturbation. Other sexual thoughts were genuinely repressed—even if only with difficulty. On a Sunday afternoon, the priest and two of his Vietnamese altar boys were away from base. The vehicle they were driving struck a land mine, and all three were mortally wounded in the explosion. Father Valour's death caused grief in a land where death had become a commonplace thing.

One popular rule of war is "Don't volunteer." Leonard

Matlovich broke the rule, and volunteered for the most dangerous missions. Not only that, he spent three tours of duty in Vietnam, practically asking to be killed. The American military policy was that after one year a veteran who had survived the conflict would never be required to return. "Only dummies like me went back," Matlovich said. "I'm still full of shrapnel everywhere. A blast blew my right lung down, literally, and it stayed down because I bled a lot internally. That blocked the lung from coming back up into its proper place.

"It was a close call. I had volunteered to work at a remote site where we thought the Vietnamese had been placing land mines the night before. Our job was to find the mines and remove them. And me, I was the perfect Polish minesweeper—I found one the hard way!

"Having only a week left in my second tour, I had decided I wasn't going to kill myself with work that day. The sun was bright, the weather hot. I walked about twenty feet away from where everybody else was carefully digging into potential danger spots. I remember finding some shade, wiping sweat from heavy-duty sunglasses I wore, and then sticking my shovel into a place in the ground where it should have stood upright. When it wouldn't, without thinking, I gave it a real hard push. It went down—and boom!

"I saw the whole thing happen. Shrapnel came up and flew right past me. Some of the small fragments that hit my sunglasses were deflected—probably saved me from being blinded. Then the next thing I knew, I was returning to consciousness, lying on the ground and looking up into concerned, sweaty faces. Smoke was everywhere, and people were running around."

Airman First Class Matlovich was too injured to travel for several weeks. He was then sent to Japan, and home to the United States for treatment. After two months, in 1967, Leonard returned to Vietnam for the third and final time. After another full year, when he finally departed from Asia, among the chest-full of citations Matlovich wore was the Bronze Star for outstanding service in battle.

There is a paper to be signed upon military enlistment, and also upon reenlistment. A question on the form asks, in essence, "Are you a homosexual?" When Leonard Matlovich answered that query in the negative, he was neither lying nor evading the truth. Not until after the commencement of his last hitch in the Air Force did Leonard come to a conclusion and admit, even to himself, "Yes, I am a homosexual."

Only during the period of his last enlistment, after nearly thirty years of celibacy, with masturbation his only confessable sexual act, did he finally accept unvarnished reality. "As an adult, looking back to the time I was four, I could realize I had always been gay, but I didn't know it then," said Leonard. "I was always fighting it—fighting it! Engaging in self-denial. Saying to myself, it's not really true—I'm going through a phase. But no matter how you try to hide it—and I was really trying to hide it—it's part of you. It's always there.

"I never slept with anyone until I was thirty. Other than members of my family, I never had the pleasure of kissing anybody. And that's a horrible life. I don't recommend it to anybody.

"I grew up always having very low self-esteem because I knew I was different. Although I couldn't consciously admit I was anything but heterosexual, when I heard the terrible things people said about 'queers,' I instinctively recoiled. I knew I never acted the way everybody said 'fags' acted, yet I constantly feared they were talking about me.

"From the time I was eleven, until seventeen—my most formative years—we lived in Charlestown, South Carolina. The Charlestown I knew was predominantly a white racist society, and I became a white racist. It happened not because I really hated anyone else, but because my own sense of self-worth was so low that, subconsciously, I figured I couldn't be such a bad person if I could put an entire race lower on the totem pole than myself."

Only with great difficulty did Matlovich manage to rid himself of the stereotypes he had been taught about people of color. His conversion occurred partly because the United States Government was having problems with black, brown, and yellow men it wanted to send off to fight for democracy. Those individuals, thinking for themselves, had begun saying, "Why me? What am I fighting for? Last week a black man who was killed fighting in Vietnam couldn't get buried in a Pensacola cemetery. Is that the democracy I want to die for? Our war for liberation is here at home! Let white men fight across the sea."

As a result, when the need arose, America's military leaders rapidly became race-conscious. After centuries of overt prejudice and discrimination in the Armed Forces, unmanageable ideas were rapidly trashed. Suddenly, on orders, black, brown, red, and yellow men and women were to be officially upgraded to human beings. And "lily-white" Leonard Matlovich, of all people, was assigned to teach race relations to help the Air Force tear down its time-tested barriers of racial prejudice!

Leonard taught the classes. He did such a splendid job in four years that he even taught himself. "I was in the closet for the first year and a half when I talked about black equality, brown equality, and how all those people had worked and struggled along with everybody else to make America a better place to live. I told my students of every color to get involved in their country and make it a better place. I said, 'If you see something wrong, have the courage of your convictions and stand up and say something.'

"While I was speaking to them about race relations, I was brainwashing myself about my own, somewhat different problem. I had actually begun to believe in the United States Constitution and the Bill of Rights. I came to believe that they really do stand for justice and equality for all. At the same time, I came to realize that not only were racial stereotypes false, but that homosexual stereotypes were probably equally incorrect. I knew I was being a hypocrite when I saw gay people being tossed out of the military and I made no effort to speak against it. I had seen some of their personnel files, and I knew that most of the gay people whom the Air Force dishonored were actually outstanding individuals, no matter what their private sexual interests.

"My own inaction was increasingly bothering my conscience. I guess I had become a starry-eyed liberal—that's a person with both feet firmly planted in the air. It was getting to the point I couldn't live with myself. I began to feel that I was a coward inside because I wasn't willing to do what I was telling other people to do. I was a do-nothing do-gooder. I felt two-faced, and one night I put an unloaded rifle to my head—but even without ammunition, I couldn't pull the trigger. There had to be a better way of solving my dilemma.

"Years later, after my picture was on the cover of *Time*, when people said to me, 'I wouldn't have the courage to come out like you did,' I replied, 'Yes, you would. Believe me, if you'd been through the self-inflicted agony I suffered, coming out would not be the hardest thing to do. I didn't just get up one morning and say, 'I'm going to fight the Air

Force.' It was a four-year process. It was a long, hard, four years of building my courage up to the point where I had to do it, where I could no longer resist exclaiming, 'No more, Air Force—it's wrong what you're doing!'"

In his race-relations classes, Sergeant Matlovich came to a point when he had the courage to initiate discussions about homosexuality. He would stand before his students and ask whom they believed to be the most discriminated-against people in America. The answers came back—blacks, women, Indians, and so forth—after which Leonard turned to a blackboard and, in letters a foot high, wrote:

HOMOSEXUALS

There would be a collective gasp. Then a debate generally followed, not from an authoritative viewpoint but with students encouraged to contribute hearsay and controversial personal viewpoints, pro and con, trying to apply the military's new standards for other forms of tolerance. "The truth is," admitted Matlovich, "I didn't know much about homosexuals. I didn't know there was a gay movement—I had never heard of gay rights. I just figured if I brought up the subject of homosexuality in the classroom, I'd get bits and pieces of information, and maybe learn more about myself.

"A student in one of my classes said that he and his wife had been driving through Pensacola, Florida (about forty miles from Eglin Air Force Base where I was stationed), and they had stopped for dinner at a show-club called the Yum Yum Tree. What they didn't know beforehand, my student said, was that the Yum Yum Tree was a gay establishment. He said the entertainers were wonderful, but not until after one of the acts when wigs were removed did he realize they were female impersonators. He also said that boys wearing only jockstraps were waiting on customers, and as the boys moved between tables, people would pull their jocks down and molest them."

Matlovich's eyes had widened as he listened to this vivid and shocking description, which tended to confirm his worst apprehensions. Nevertheless, once he knew the location of such a place, it was inevitable he would want to have a look for himself. Never in his life had he seen the inside of a gay bar or restaurant.

"After thinking about it a lot," said Leonard, "I had to find out for myself what a gay club's like. I had a three-quarter-ton truck at the time, with big snow tires—in northwest Florida where it almost never snows! I parked the truck five blocks away from the club so nobody could connect my vehicle with a homosexual establishment, and hiked the distance from one to the other.

"At the Yum Yum Tree, I was like a yo-yo, trying to look casual as I walked back and forth, having great difficulty mustering the courage to enter. Inside the building, there was a long L-shaped hallway you had to traverse before actually entering the club. I took a couple of steps down that corridor and then fled. A few minutes later, I forced myself to walk a few steps further, before again retreating. Finally, I summoned the courage to turn the corner, and walked inside."

What a shock—and one of the most important and pleasant surprises in Leonard's thirty years! It was a mixed bar, with gay men and lesbians. All of them were adults. No children (nearly naked, molested, or otherwise) were present, and never had been. "After all the terrible stories I had ever heard about 'queers' and 'perverts,'" smiled Leonard, "seeing the real thing was so totally different. In an instant, a billion pounds of pressure fell from my shoulders! For the next two hours I didn't talk to anyone. I just walked around the bar and the restaurant, sipping ginger ale, as I watched homosexual people—good-looking men and women—enjoying life in pleasant surroundings!

"I was just amazed to see those wonderful smiling people, laughing, dancing, and being themselves. I said to myself, I'm going to get out of the Air Force and become a happy civilian like everybody else. About then I sat down, and the first person I talked to turned out to be the president of a bank. He told me that in his private life he had problems and fears similar to my own, so I decided to remain in the Air Force. Why should I leave a job I really liked if civilians had the same difficulties?

"'No way!' I said to myself.

"In a few hours I had gone from darkness into the light. I had seen firsthand that gay people are not awful stereotypes as portrayed by society and the military. Anyone with an open mind and eyes to see could observe that beneath the bravado we are good people who contribute to the world of which we're a part. The idea of homosexuals being synonymous with child abusers and molesters became a patently false generalization.

"That night I made a commitment to fight."

A few months later, an article about homosexuals in the military appeared in *The Air Force Times*. From the story, Matlovich obtained the name of a civilian astronomer in Washington, D.C., who had been steadily fighting antigay practices in the civil service and the military, particularly concerning himself with those institutions' refusal to hire, retain, or grant security clearances to homosexual men and women. His name was Franklin E. Kameny.

Matlovich telephoned Washington. "Dr. Kameny," he

said, "I'm a sergeant in the Air Force, and I teach race relations. Every so often, in every class, we talk about homosexuality. What can you tell me?"

As it turned out, Kameny had much to tell. He and Matlovich spoke for hours, and during that conversation, Kameny made an extremely fateful statement. He mentioned that he and his associates were looking for a person in the United States Armed Forces, a person with special qualifications, including, primarily, an unblemished record. They wanted an exemplary individual who could legally challenge the military's policy toward homosexuals.

Just as Leonard was about to hang up at the end of the conversation, as if in an afterthought (although it was not), he said, "What type of person did you say you're looking for?"

Kameny replied, "Either a man or a woman who'll admit to being gay, and who wants to stay in the military."

After a moment of hesitation, the sergeant replied, "Well, Frank, I have someone in mind for you. Let me talk to that person and see what he says."

The person, of course, was himself, Technical Sergeant Leonard P. Matlovich. And if there was any doubt that Matlovich was destined to challenge the Air Force in court, he was fortuitously transferred from the Air Force Base outside of Pensacola, Florida, to Langley Air Force Base in Hampton, Virginia—less than a hundred and fifty miles from Washington, D.C., and within commuting distance of Frank Kameny and others (including Attorney David Addlestone of the American Civil Liberties Union) who were interested in testing the military's entrenched homophobic discrimination.

Matlovich had been made the top noncommissioned officer teaching race relations for Tactical Air Command, and as such traveled all over the United States to air bases where it was his duty to be certain racial programs were up to command standards. He had much to lose by telling the Air Force what they were not prepared to hear.

Nevertheless, Matlovich told Kameny and Addlestone, "I'm your man. I've been in service twelve years, and I'm gay. I have never been in trouble. I have a Bronze Star, a Purple Heart, and three Commendations for performance above and beyond the call of duty. On the Air Force's quarterly rating scale of 1 to a top of 9, I have never received less than 9 in my entire enlistment. Now I want to end the military's prejudice against homosexuality, and I'm willing to fight all the way to the Supreme Court of the United States if it's necessary!"

"A beautiful case," said Addlestone, but Frank Kameny discouraged the airman. Older and wiser, Kameny had long fought bigotry-bound governmental policies, and almost single-handed, was responsible for the civil service changing its rules so that government employees could no longer be fired strictly on the basis of being gay. Very many owe very much to Frank Kameny. Yet, the homosexual gadfly did not want to destroy an individual, even for a commendable cause. Kameny knew the dangers of defeat. Also, Kameny wanted to be assured of Matlovich's commitment.

"We agreed to fight all the way to the bitter end," recalled Leonard. "Then we planned and planned, and I think much of the planning was intended to keep me from losing my cool. I only had eight more years to go until retirement. That could be flushed down the drain. And I thought once my parents found out about me, I would never see them again. So it wasn't an easy step. About a year passed before we decided I was ready to not only break down the door but to destroy my closet forever. I recall that it was a Thursday in March when I went up to Washington and we wrote my letter to the Air Force."

On the ensuing Saturday morning, Sergeant Matlovich neared his point of no return. That fateful day, instead of catching a hop to the Midwest on Air Force business, he walked into the office of his boss, Captain Carlings, a black man. The captain was standing near his desk when the sergeant said, "Captain, I have something I want you to read, and I think you ought to sit down."

"No, Sergeant," the captain said, "I'll stand."

Matlovich tightened his grip on the paper he was holding, fully aware that the letter between his fingers was, literally, his career. There was nothing except nervous, burning determination to prevent him from simply turning and running away. But he held his ground. He said, "Really, Captain, I think you ought to sit down."

"No, I'll stand," insisted the officer.

Matlovich hesitated.

The captain glared.

It was time to quit the meaningless jousting. Matlovich thrust a hand forward with his candid, straight-from-the-shoulder letter. Impatiently, Captain Carlings took it!

The officer unsealed the envelope. Carlings read the first paragraph quickly, then decided he would take a seat after all, and began reading again. When he had finished, he looked up. With intonations of disbelief and anger, he read a sentence from Leonard's letter aloud, "'I have arrived at the conclusion that my sexual preferences are homosexual as opposed to heterosexual.' Sergeant, what does this mean?" he demanded.

"It means 'Brown versus the Board of Education,'" replied Matlovich, unready to give a direct response, knowing the black officer, a senior race relations instructor,

would understand that by quoting the name of the land-
mark civil rights case, he was indicating to a knowledgeable person that he, too, meant to fight discrimination.

A spectacular military lawyer was appointed to represent Matlovich in addition to Addlestone and Hewman,
his civilian counsel. "By sheer luck," Leonard said, "I got
Captain Janeke, an intellectual fellow who had joined the
Air Force during the war to keep out of the Army. Janeke hated the military, and told me ahead of time about
ways they had to prejudice a case. 'What's more, Tech,'
he said, 'this will probably happen. One day, the colonel
will stop by and say to you, very offhandedly, that he forgot to tell you yesterday, but you're wanted for a little
interrogation—now! They'll try to catch you off guard.
Don't let it happen.' As a result, when exactly what was
predicted occurred, I was ready.

"I'd seen firsthand what the military can do to an individual. Their justice is better on paper than the civilian system,
but the trouble is that the military doesn't always follow their
system. They jockey it around, trying to make the boss
happy, and if the boss is a four-star tyrant with everybody incredibly afraid of him, what can you expect? The truth—but
only if that's what the general wants."

Relieved of duty as an instructor, Matlovich was relegated to an undemanding assignment, in charge of bar-
racks at Langley. His first sergeant, twenty years older
than Leonard and definitely among the enemy, was quick
to say, "I'd get rid of a faggot like you, Matlovich. I'd say
you were staring at men in the showers—propositioning
young recruits—making everybody uncomfortable. You'd
be out on your ear so fast your head would spin!'

"But the Air Force thought twice about setting me up,"
said Leonard, "because of television and radio and newspapers. I knew because the first sergeant could never keep his

mouth shut. He told me they were afraid of the adverse publicity if they were caught doing something dirty."

In the evening of the same Saturday when he gave Captain Carlings his letter telling the Air Force that he was homosexual, Sgt. Matlovich called home. His mother answered the telephone. After nearly an hour of stammering and stuttering, Leonard came around to nervously telling her what he had told the military. "My mother," remembers Leonard, "having been brainwashed in the great tradition of the Irish Catholics, exclaimed, 'God is punishing me! That's why you're like this!'

"I said what I could to soothe her and, eventually, when she calmed down, I was able to say. 'Well, we're going to have to tell Dad.'

"That brought another outburst. 'Oh, no! No, no, no!' Mother immediately replied. 'Don't tell your father! He'll blame me because you're that way, and he'll throw me out of the house!' She was terrified. I realized how formidable my extremely conservative father, a strict Catholic with thirty-two years in the Air Force, could be! My mother's fear was absolutely real, and because she believed it, I believed it. So we didn't tell my father."

In the beginning, Leonard did not anticipate a flood of publicity. He had little idea of what might happen, being primarily concerned with what he thought of as a simple injustice that reasonable people could correct. But in June, someone leaked his story to *The New York Times*, and upon advice of counsel, Matlovich agreed to give the *Times'* reporters an interview. They flew to Virginia to meet him. Not long afterward, as promised, a woman reporter called and told the sergeant that his story would break either on Sunday, or the following Monday, which was Memorial Day, 1975.

On Sunday, Leonard went to a newsstand. *The New York Times* was there, but his story was not. The next day, Leonard returned. Again, there was *The New York Times,* folded in half. He picked it up, turned it—and saw his own picture staring at him—from the front page!

Minutes after Leonard arrived back at quarters, his telephone began ringing. A man from California said, "I'm with *The Advocate.* We want to interview you."

"What's *The Advocate?*" asked Matlovich.

"A national gay newspaper," answered a surprised voice.

"Oh, wow!" exclaimed Leonard. He had not been aware that such a publication existed.

NBC Television was soon on the telephone. "We've sent for a helicopter, and we're flying down to interview you for the national news tonight," they told him.

"I have to get an okay from my lawyers," said Sergeant Matlovich.

"We already have it," said NBC.

Leonard began to feel a little panicky. He knew his father usually watched NBC's nightly news, so he quickly telephoned home. His parents' line gave him a busy signal for half an hour. When he was able to get through, his mother answered. He said desperately, "We have to tell Dad now! NBC's coming here to interview me for television, and we have to tell him I'm gay. I don't want him to learn it on the six o'clock news!"

Leonard's mother, unlike before, was infuriatingly calm. She said, "It's not necessary to tell him."

"Why?" asked Leonard, with terrible possibilities jumping into his mind.

"Your father already knows," said his mother.

"You told him?" asked Leonard, incredulous.

"No, he read it. It's on the front of *The Palm Beach Post!*"

You know he reads his paper first thing every morning!"

The sergeant dropped his head, beginning to feel warm and mildly sick to his stomach. He knew almost nothing about media operations. He had never realized his first interview would be in any paper but *The New York Times*, which was unlikely to be read by his family in Florida. He had never imagined that other newspapers would have an interest in him, and would take his story from a wire service.

"Your father got the paper before breakfast this morning, and there you were on the front page," Leonard's mother continued. "He couldn't eat. He went to his room and cried for a couple of hours."

Matlovich steeled himself for the worst. He expected to be told that he would never be welcome at home again.

"Your father has something to say to you now," said Leonard's mother. Leonard thought he discerned a warning in her voice. When the elder Matlovich came on the line, he had arrived at irrevocable conclusions. There was no indecision. He said what he thought—but what he thought was a complete reversal of what Leonard expected.

The sergeant's father was a champion. He said, "Lenny, I don't understand this, and I'm not happy with it. But I trust you realize what you're doing, and we know you've thought it through. You wouldn't do it if it wasn't right. So fight! Go ahead, son. Stand up for what you believe and fight the Air Force. I know from experience they're sometimes wrong, and I support you all the way. When it gets tough, don't ever forget the most important thing—we love you!"

Leonard, who had momentarily forgotten to breathe, began to inhale again. "You'll never know," he said, wiping away tears that came quickly to his eyes, "how much that means to me."

As Technical Sergeant Matlovich awaited trial, there were numerous telephone calls with his father, mother, sister, and nieces. From them he received support which, although it had not been anticipated, was greatly appreciated. During one of the calls, his father, having realized that Leonard had been withdrawn from his parents for many years because of his secret, said, "I wish you had told me a long time ago." His mother said the same thing, adding, "We could have gotten you help."

Leonard laughed. "In that case," he recalled later, "I'm so glad I didn't tell them, because I know how persistent my mother could be. She really would have sent me seeking 'help,' making certain I was corrected the 'good moral way,' the Catholic way, and there's no telling how screwed up I'd be today!

"My mother is a very private person, and the publicity, all of which caught us unawares, bothered her greatly. Any kind of public display is not to her liking. If I had been elected President of the United States, she would have hated the loss of our privacy. But with an uncommon name like Matlovich, even when she used her credit cards, signed a check or anything like that, people would recognize our name, and stare at mother, or make comments. She hated that.

"On one occasion, she told me that my father had asked her, 'What do they do in bed?' and she replied to him, 'Why are you asking me? I don't know.' You'd think that after thirty-two years in the Air Force he could have figured it out."

The five officers (majors and colonels) that sat on Sergeant Matlovich's trial also professed in court to have little understanding of the sexual subject. Two of the commissioned officers were obviously homophobic and would be dismissed before the trial's conclusion. Only one admitted to having read much about homosexuality; his sources were *Playboy* and *Reader's Digest.*

Matlovich was tried on two precise and limited issues: that he had violated Air Force Regulation 39-12, which states "homosexuality is not tolerated," and the Uniform Code of Military Justice's Article 125, which prohibits "unnatural copulation." The sergeant admitted to both! His defense was on the grounds that Regulation 39-12 was unconstitutional because it required unequal treatment, and that Article 125 was also unconstitutional because it was not in any way applied to essentially identical practices as commonly performed by heterosexuals. The latter point was driven home by Attorney Susan Hewman when the Lieutenant Colonel in charge of base security unwittingly testified that heterosexual adultery, heterosexual fellatio, heterosexual cunnilingus, heterosexual sodomy, wife-swapping, et cetera, also fell within the province of Article 125 of the Uniform Code of Military Justice, but were construed as "minor sexual matters" and were "never" given official notice in nongay situations!

Expert witnesses called by the defense explained some basic facts. Dr. Wardell Pomeroy, a coauthor of *Sexual Behavior in the Human Male,* popularly known as the Kinsey Report, testified, "We've chosen to define homosexuality as immoral, but society is now in the process of making up its mind whether this long-standing stigma any longer makes any sense—just as it has recently made up its mind to take mad people out of dungeons, and to stop treating left-handedness as a disease."

John Money, head of a research unit at John Hopkins and president of the Society for the Scientific Study of Sex, testified that a convincing variety of studies have demonstrated that an individual's sexual orientation cannot be altered, at the latest, after the age of five.

Near the end of the trial, Sergeant Matlovich, a decidedly sympathetic defendant, could have been retained in the Air Force, which, by its own regulations, allowed for exceptions under "extraordinary circumstances"—if he had taken what would have amounted to a vow of chastity—if (as figuratively asserted in a magazine article in *The New York Times*) he had agreed to wear an inwardly "spiked penile ring guaranteed to discourage any threat of tumescence"!

"Sergeant Matlovich," the prosecution asked, "will you sign a contract never to practice homosexuality again?"

"No, I will not," was his unwavering response.

To the Air Force, Matlovich was automatically guilty. Constitutional arguments be damned! Later, Leonard admitted, "Losing had the benefit of allowing an appeal. If I had been successful at Langley, it wouldn't have settled anything. Besides, television that protected me would have gone away—and since I was no longer the Air Force's favorite son, they would have crucified me! I was well aware that the first sergeant, or somebody with his mentality, would have me court-martialed, perhaps the very next day, on any trumped-up provocation. I'd have been finished, and for nothing. As it was, I thought I had an opportunity to appeal my case all the way to the United States Supreme Court. My ambition was to correct the law."

Matlovich's first appeal, following his discharge, went to the district court in Washington, D.C. There, Judge Gerhard Gazelle indicated he thought that the Air Force, in view of the decorated sergeant's record, should reconsider its decision, but beyond his own personal opinion, Gazelle saw nothing in the Constitution that barred the military from discharging homosexuals. With District

Judge Gazelle's ruling in favor of the Air Force, the American Civil Liberties Union washed its hands of Matlovich's case. Their rationale was that they had decided Leonard no longer had a chance of winning reinstatement. The ACLU was sensitive about the possibility that losing a case might result in the creation of "bad law" that could be detrimental to their objectives.

Matlovich, however, was not ready to quit. Disappointed that his legal friends were shedding what he considered their obligation to him, he struck out on his own and found a new attorney, Gary Bogan from New York City, and together, they went to the United States Court of Appeals.

"It was wonderful!" exclaimed Leonard.

There were three judges on the court. A lawyer from the Department of Justice argued for the military. He said that under no circumstances could a homosexual serve in the Armed Forces, but admitted that there was an "exception for extraordinary circumstances." Whereupon, the three court of appeals judges said to the Department of Justice lawyer, "We have Matlovich's military record before us. It's absolutely flawless! Why doesn't he qualify to be the extraordinary exception to the regulations? And just for the record, exactly what is the exception to the regulations?"

"The exception," replied the Justice Department's lawyer, "is anything the Secretary of the Air Force says is the exception."

"You mean to tell us," asked one of the irritated judges, "that if the Secretary of the Air Force says brown-eyed homosexuals can serve, and blue-eyed homosexuals cannot, *that* is the exception to the regulations?"

"Yes," said the lawyer.

"No! No! No!" said the judges, "We don't agree with

you—not at all! We're sending this case back to Judge
Gazelle for reconsideration."

So the case was returned to the lower court, where
Judge Gazelle, over and over again, asked the Secretary
of the Air Force, "What is the exception to the regulations?" But the Secretary of the Air Force repeatedly ignored requests for an answer, causing the judge to
seriously consider finding him in contempt of court.

Finally, without ever receiving an enlightening response, the frustrated judge made his ruling. "I'm not
saying the military can't discharge homosexuals," he said.
"I'm saying there must be a standard policy as to why a
person does, or does not, meet an exception to the regulations. They have to tell you why you don't meet their
exception when they throw you out. And since the Air
Force won't, or can't, tell this court, I'm ordering Matlovich reinstated into the military, and he is to receive all
back pay, plus a promotion."

A victory by default!

There was no win on constitutional grounds, but not
for the want of trying. "The military said they would pay
me $160,000 not to return to duty," said Matlovich, "and
my lawyers, everybody, wanted me to take it. If I had
never admitted to committing sexual acts, and, if like
Jimmy Carter, I had only 'lusted in my mind,' I might
have won. But I had made the mistake of admitting to
having committed sodomy, which in the military, as in
some of the states, is against the law when applied to homosexuals. I could only take some degree of satisfaction
in our defeat by setting the precedent of taking their
money, which we did.

"The truth is, I no longer wanted back in the Air
Force. By 1979, I was a changed person."

Homosexuals are still not fairly treated in the Armed Forces, but to a great extent because of the publicity in Sergeant Matlovich's struggle, lesbians and gay men who have committed no criminal offense are now released with a fully honorable discharge. "Upstanding gay men or lesbians who were previously let go with anything less than an honorable discharge," explains Leonard Matlovich, "should take action now to obtain an upgrade, and do it no matter how many years—twenty, thirty, forty or whatever—have passed. Correcting the old injustices is important to our struggle, and there are many organizations that will help—Swords Into Plowshares, the Gay Rights National Lobby, and others. It's very routine. Just do the paperwork, and your discharge comes back upgraded.

"I think everyone must leave the closet sometime. I'm not the person to harm those that are not ready by dragging them out, but I think they are hurting us all by not coming forward. There are some exceptions. If we found that somebody like Jerry Falwell was secretly gay, in such a case we'd have a moral obligation to drag him, kicking and screaming, out of the closet. Rock Hudson came halfway out, without admitting it. Liberace could have done incalculable good! Coming out is the only way to end prejudice, and we should fight it, and fight it, and fight it. Everyone should come out, including the four-star general.

"But if a person feels that he or she must stay in the military, there is no choice—you must lie. I couldn't live under those conditions, but it's up to the individual. If you're identified, they may come to you with a blank piece of paper and say they have on it the names of fifteen people who've seen you engaged in sex. Don't fall for their tricks to make you confess. Give nothing but name, rank, and serial number—and get a good lawyer! Those are your constitutional rights.

"Before I came out of the closet, I would have rather not been gay. If I'd had a choice then, I'd have chosen to be heterosexual. Now that I know what gay life really is, I would choose it. Being openly gay has made me a better person with more depth. I can see through a lot of dishonesty.

"Many people in the military today are educated enough so they know what's going on, but they ignore it. Usually the attitude is, 'Don't tell me about it.' However, the problem with that is, one day you might have a good commanding officer, and the next day may bring another C.O. who's a vicious son-of-a-bitch.

"Rough constitutional battles lie ahead that need to be won. The false arguments against having uncloseted gays serving their country are ingrained, despite a proven lack of validity. For instance, we are libelously and slander-ously called security risks. Can you imagine anyone black-mailing me? How could they do it?

"I have always been basically old-fashioned. What I wanted was a yard with a picket fence, a dog, a cat, and a lover, not necessarily in that order. I never had a lover, and now it's unlikely that I ever will. Having AIDS is a curse as well as a blessing. The curse is that I am not well. The blessing is that I can leave with a feeling that the world's a better place. There are people who are better off because I existed.

"We are all parents, every gay man and every lesbian, whether we have biological children or not. Our children are tomorrow's generations of gays and lesbians who are coming along. We have to give them roots. We have to sac-rifice today, as all parents do, to give them a better world. I think that because of you, Tom, and Troy, and me—all of us in the last forty years—the world is a better place.

"We are good parents.

"We care about tomorrow."

New Thoughts
on Unthinkable Subjects

~~~~~~

It rained without warning in Chicago on Thursday, the
week before Thanksgiving in 1949. Barbara Gittings
pulled her coat close, unable to ignore a downpour as
she stepped off the train that brought her from college.
Without an umbrella, she sloshed through windy streets,
keeping water off her head with a thoroughly soaked
magazine of mystery and science fiction. Half an hour
later, seated in a nondescript waiting room, Barbara felt
her heart pounding. The doctor was late, unusual for a
psychiatrist.

Already mildly uneasy, Barbara was considering a fast
exit when a receptionist appeared in the doorway. "Miss
Gittings," said the matron with a professional smile, "will
you come in now?"

The psychiatrist, a woman, was all business—but that
suited her seventeen-year-old client, who would pay for
the visit out of her allowance. "You're a freshman at
Northwestern?" asked the doctor.

"Yes."

"And you've had some trouble?"

"No, but they say I'm homosexual," answered Barbara frankly, pausing a moment before adding, "I don't know if I am. My girlfriend at school won't see me anymore—because of what's been said. I want to find out if it's true. And how other students can know, if I don't know myself?"

Venetian blinds filtered the washed sunlight coming into the office. Specks of dust floated across diagonal sunbeams. Behind her desk, the doctor interlaced her fingers and spoke in a trained monotone. "You have to relax," she said. "I'll listen, and you will put before me the evidence of your life. When you're done, I'll give you an answer if that is possible."

Barbara agreed, and settled into a comfortable leather chair as she began telling her story. She had been born in Vienna, where her father, a secretary in the American diplomatic service, was stationed until he returned with his family to North America. Early memories were of North Carolina, Maryland, and Canada—and of going to strict Catholic schools with her sister and brother. After completing seventh grade, Barbara chose to enter a public school.

"I had no dislike for boys," Barbara told the psychiatrist, "but in high school, I felt a special kind of interest for girls. After graduation, I wanted to go to California to study drama, but my father said it was too far and would cost too much. So I came to Northwestern instead. I became a friend, just a friend, with one girl particularly liked. That's when the whispering began. Now my girlfriend is frightened—and keeps her distance from me—as if we'd done something wrong."

Barbara detailed more of her life, answering questions

until, after a time, she hesitated and looked up into the doctor's eyes. "So tell me," she said, "am I a homosexual, or not?"

"You are definitely homosexual," the psychiatrist replied.

There was no equivocation.

Later, a friend declared, "That psychiatrist shouldn't have labeled you."

"On the contrary," replied Barbara, "she did me a favor by giving me the information—and I appreciated it—although I never returned to her office. Sure, she put a tag on me, and proposed to 'cure' me with extensive—and expensive—psychotherapy. But at least the penny dropped. I knew who I was. I was a homosexual. And that was fine. My next step was that I had to find out what being homosexual meant! Homosexuality was a mystery as far as I was concerned, and solving that mystery became a consuming desire.

"At that time, most newspapers wouldn't print the word *homosexual,* much less discuss anything about it of a positive nature. Nor was homosexuality considered a subject for polite discussion, even among friends. Television shows wouldn't touch the topic. Visible gay role models didn't exist. So, I very soon discovered, my path toward better understanding was actually leading me into badly charted territory."

There were few signposts. Bits of information in libraries were, more often than not, brief, subjective, and grim. Nevertheless, in her desperation, books became a primary resource for Barbara, even as her attendance at university classes ceased (with the exception of singing in the Glee Club, which she dearly loved). Instead of scheduled classes, Barbara went to all of Northwestern's campus libraries, including those for medicine and law, and after laboriously mining them for their meager information, she traveled to a variety of public libraries in and around Chicago.

"Some people naturally gravitate toward books," said Barbara, "and I have always been that way. I started looking at everything on the subject of homosexuality that I could get my hands on. Some of it was pretty weird! I remember reading that the majority of homosexuals have the same favorite color—green. My favorite color at the time was blue, and I didn't know what to make of that.

"There were psychologists who wasted an inordinate amount of time comparing the penile measurements of homosexuals with similar parts of heterosexual males. There were no overall differences, but the researchers seemed engrossed in their work.

"It was necessary," continued Barbara, "to spend a tremendous amount of time just searching for homosexual topics in print, even though there usually was not much substance. Nevertheless, every encyclopedia was rifled by me for tidbits of information. And I was not deterred in my quest even by the necessity of looking up homosexuality under such headings as 'abnormal,' 'perverted,' or 'deviate.'

"Most literature before and including the Fifties concerned gay men, not gay women, but that really didn't bother me, I was so hungry for the information. Besides, although I was certain the research material was intended to be about persons like myself, I innately knew the majority of clinical studies were erroneous. Researchers were usually missing the mark by attempting to shoehorn their subjects into preconceived, odd little categories. Homosexuals, clinically described, didn't sound anything like me.

"My greatest objection was that the professional, pseudomedical writing never mentioned the subject of love.

And I wondered, doesn't love have anything to do with my life? Doesn't love have something to do with being homosexual? I had been attracted to several girls, and I knew that, unless I was terribly mistaken, elements of love had been involved. My feelings for girls were not unlike the feelings other girls were having for boys. There was an unmistakable similarity.

"My first breakthrough came when I found some fiction, the novels of homosexuality, books often banned and difficult to obtain. They were like a breath of fresh air compared with the dismal, clinical reading I'd been absorbing. In the novels, at last, were stories about fairly realistic, flesh-and-blood characters, men and women in recognizable situations. They were believable people who had feelings, who lived, loved, and had their moments of happiness, people with whom it was at least possible to identify—using reasonable stretches of the imagination. And never mind the fact that the novels almost always had unhappy endings.

"As my search continued, locating material on homosexuality occupied most of my time. Other studies were just incidental. That showed my priorities. I had no thought other than to solve the riddle of who I was, and the problem of what my life was going to be."

When the college semester ended, and failing grades for Barbara were posted, she returned home. The fact that hers was not a free-talking family worked to Barbara's advantage. There was little discussion about her academic failure. However, on another matter Barbara's father would in his own way have a say.

His letter addressed to Barbara arrived in the mail, which most people would find strange since father and daughter were both living in the same house at the same time. Mr. Gittings' letter stated that a novel, *The Well of*

Loneliness, had been discovered in Barbara's bedroom. (Discovery must have been a feat, because Barbara's room was anything but orderly. Nevertheless, the father's concern was only about the novel.) He was writing about its discovery, he explained, because he could not bring himself to discuss it face-to-face. The gist of his message was that the lesbian love story was immoral trash and that Barbara was under his injunction not to pass it on to anybody else because they might be contaminated by its contents. Furthermore, the book was to be burned— immediately!

"So I hid it better," said Barbara, "and he never found it again. But the signs of my homosexuality were beginning to add up, and that worried my father." It never became an issue, however, because before long Barbara left home to fend for herself in Philadelphia. Much of the support she carried with her was derived from lesbians in fiction. And whatever they might have lacked in the eyes of critics, extraordinary heroines made Barbara feel better about herself. And the search for books continued.

When Barbara discovered an extensive listing of novels in the back of Donald Webster Cory's *The Homosexual in America,* she did more than try to obtain the mentioned volumes; she telephoned Cory's publisher, made contact with the author, and visited with him in his New York City home, where they discussed homosexual literature on more than one occasion.

"A lot of titles on Cory's list of additional reading material had come to him secondhand from mentions by old-time sexologists, and I discovered that the homosexual element in some books was really obscure, if there at all. But I only learned by actually obtaining the volumes, purchasing them from dusty bookstores or looking them up in libraries. Needless to say, books with explicit homosexual themes were the most appealing to me.

"In those days I had a lot of hours for myself, and I spent a lot of time hunting for books to add to my collection. When I found a new book, it was almost always read. The jobs I had made no demands. I worked as a sales clerk in a music store and, at another time, was employed by a wholesale florist where they had me running back and forth in the racks hauling cartons of flowers—it was a great job!"

During one of Barbara's meetings with Cory, he told her of bona fide gay organizations that had been established a few years previously, but which she had never suspected existed: ONE, Inc. and the Mattachine Society, both located in California. Barbara determined to go west! When she did, members of San Francisco's Mattachine Society helpfully referred Barbara on to a pioneering lesbian organization formed without fanfare the year before. Within hours of hearing about it, Barbara located the group and attended her first meeting with the Daughters of Bilitis.

It was a small get-together. Held in a member's living room, fourteen women were present, including two of the founders, Phyllis Lyon and Del Martin. Phyl and Del would eventually become famous in the gay and lesbian community for their leadership activities—including feminist sociopolitical advances, battling against gay and non-gay male chauvinism, and defeating psychiatric obstinacy. When Barbara Gittings first met the couple, in 1956, Del was the first elected president of Daughters of Bilitis, and Phyl was the original editor of the group's publication *The Ladder,* which Phyl and Del would soon evolve into a national lesbian magazine.

So easily and naturally did Barbara take to the pleasant company that she was dismayed to find herself, an outspoken newcomer, unable to resist being brashly critical of the organization's name. "Bilitis is hard to pronounce if you haven't heard it before," she said. "Bilitis was a fictional character. And besides all that, she was bisexual—not really a lesbian."

The name, nevertheless, continued unchanged.

Two years later, Barbara was a founder of the New York City chapter of Daughters of Bilitis, and she was elected to be that chapter's first president, a position she held for three years, until 1961, the same year she met Kay Tobin Lahusen. Kay would be a future cofounder of the Gay Activists Alliance in New York, coauthor of a biographical anthology titled *The Gay Crusaders,* cofounder of Gay Women's Alternative, and Barbara's continuing friend and lover. Between the two of them, they have managed more often than not to charm both advocates and adversaries.

Two years after Kay and Barbara met, Barbara was asked to become editor of *The Ladder,* even though it was published in San Francisco and she and Kay had their home in Philadelphia. Phyllis and Del had given ample warning that they wanted to step down from editorial responsibilities they had shared for years, but no one had stepped forward to take their places. Thus, with some reluctance, Gittings consented to helm the only lesbian magazine of its day—"only for a few months"—until an editor could be found in the San Francisco area.

"But the months turned into years," said Barbara, breaking into a sunny grin, "and I kept the job because I found that I liked being editor. I liked the power. Suddenly I had a new way of expressing things. Not that I wrote editorials or articles for the magazine—I wasn't good at that. But I understood how to use the prerogative of an editor—to choose, to deliberately seek what needed to be written. Although Kay's name didn't appear on the masthead, her vision, as much as mine, shaped the magazine for three and a half years. It was Kay who introduced photographic portraits of real lesbians on the cover of *The Ladder,* a historic breakthrough.

"As part of my drive to build a closer relationship with our best authors, I visited Barbara Grier in Kansas City. Grier, under the pseudonym Gene Damon, regularly supplied *The Ladder* with capsulized book reviews in a column called 'Lesbiana.' To my dismay, I discovered that she had a large collection of gay books that beat my library hands down! There was no contest. My respectable accumulation would have looked anemic compared to Grier's, which, to the best of my knowledge, was the most extensive private collection of lesbian literature in America."

Consequently, although Barbara continued to collect books, her principal energies refocused on the specific objectives of creating a national, lesbian magazine. "I kept trying to print controversial issues that seemed important to what was, in the early Sixties, still a small, scattered gay movement," Barbara explained. "In one issue of *The Ladder,* I presented the pros and the cons of actively demonstrating for the gay cause even though I knew a significant number of our readers believed picketing was a tactic that would tarnish our image. They preferred the more cautious path of public education, coupled with low-profile efforts at legislative reform."

Indeed, a majority of homosexuals believed that shouting slogans of liberation and carrying signs in the streets was somehow similar to being unpatriotic. They rationalized that such public protests were best left to groups not connected with the movement. As one of Barbara's readers declared, "Only the dirty, unwashed rabble do that sort of thing!"

"In those early days of the gay movement," said Gittings, "our public image was, understandably, a matter of particular concern. We were not popular. Our cause was not popular. And we knew that better than anyone. It was, therefore, important not to be dismissed from consideration before our messages could be heard.

"There were factions in our movement who wanted to break all barriers. As a result, tension existed. The resulting conflict, with merit on both sides, was the basis for various provocative articles which provided *The Ladder*'s readership (less than two hundred subscribers plus perhaps a thousand persons who passed copies from hand to hand) with food for thought. Keeping that in mind, Kay and I believed we could eventually reach tens of thousands of lesbians who had never heard about our movement, lesbians who didn't necessarily want to join us but needed to see themselves in a better light, who needed to know they were not alone, that something was being done to change things.

"We succeeded in convincing Daughters of Bilitis to allow an important modification to our magazine so that henceforth its name would read, *The Ladder—A Lesbian Review*. Openly using the word *lesbian* was tremendously significant! It meant that *The Ladder* was finally out of the closet. Anybody who saw the magazine would henceforth know who we were, what we were about, and how to reach us, which turned out not to be a bad thing."

Furthermore, in a trailblazing attempt to bolster circulation, Barbara and Kay made valiant efforts to have *The Ladder* sold by quality bookstores. But resistance to selling a gay publication was frustrating and depressing in the Sixties. Just walking into a store and asking if they would display an esoteric twenty-eight-page literary magazine of interest to lesbians required maximum courage!

Barbara or Kay would brace themselves, swallow their fears, and say, "Look, here's a good magazine that we're producing. We are certain many women will want to buy and read it, and we'd like you to sell some copies." There was never any way of predicting a bookstore manager's reaction. Most often it was a definite "not interested."

"But we did get some acceptances," Barbara remembers. "We finally found a couple of bookstores in Philadelphia, and one in all of Manhattan, that agreed to carry *The Ladder*. Today that may not sound like much. At the time, it was a major breakthrough. We had a celebration because it was the first time our magazine would be offered for sale—not in a gay bar—not from under the counter—not in some private place—but openly to the general public. Visibility would increase magazine circulation, and the message of hope would begin trickling through to people that didn't yet know our community existed."

In the years preceding the 1969 Stonewall Rebellion, what was still a small gay movement was beginning to grow. Barbara Gittings was one of only a handful of people who participated in the early pickets, protests, meetings, and legal challenges of those years. In 1964, at a conference of East Coast Homophile Organizations, Barbara met Dr. Franklin E. Kameny, a prominent gay activist who was to affect her life deeply.

Dr. Kameny was a brilliant physicist-astronomer who, because federal agents had viciously disrupted his life, boldly transformed himself into a gay activist of major importance. Kameny had been summarily fired from a civil service position in which he made sky surveys for the Army Map Service. His curt dismissal for being homosexual was not related to job performance. Following four years of frustrating legal battles for reinstatement, his

self-written brief reached the United States Supreme
Court in 1961; but the high court rejected Kameny's appeal. Thereafter, to the considerable chagrin of holier-
than-thou federal busybodies, Frank embarked upon a
crusade against his government's pervasive antigay policies in both military and civilian areas of jurisdiction, do-
nating much of his time to the counseling of gay people
whom the Department of Defense and the Civil Service
Commission were victimizing with impunity. Very often,
Kameny, a fast learner, enabled others to win cases similar to those he had not won for himself.

In his brief for the U.S. Supreme Court, Kameny had
written, "In World War Two, petitioner did not hesitate
to fight the Germans, with bullets, in order to help preserve his rights and freedoms and liberties—and those of
others. Now it is ironic but necessary that he fight Americans, with words, in order to preserve some of those same
rights, freedoms, and liberties for himself and others.

"As an employer, the government's only proper concern is with the employee's work and conduct during
working hours. It is not for the government-as-employer
to intercede in the employee's private affairs. These are
matters between the employee himself and his conscience. Our government exists to protect and assist *all* of
its citizens, not, as in the case of homosexuals, to harm,
to victimize, and to destroy them."

The brief marked a time when knowledgeable homosexuals were beginning to dispute insupportable psychiatric claptrap repeatedly dispensed by anti-gay segments of
the medical profession; and Frank was among the first to
formulate and verbalize a dynamic challenge to the prejudicial "sickness" label then in vogue. In the absence of
scientific evidence to the contrary, he declared homosexuality is a healthy state fully equal to, and on a par with,
heterosexuality.

Barbara Gittings agreed, and was pleased to feature what Kameny wrote for publication in the pages of *The Ladder.* That precipitated a vigorous exchange of ideas because, in effect, Barbara was encouraging an evolution from Daughters of Bilitis' fundamental philosophy of (1) "education of the variant" and (2) "education of the public" to a considerably more radical agenda, self-assertion by gay people, and rough and tumble political activism. In the May 1965 issue of *The Ladder,* Kameny contributed the following summary of his position.

"There was, and is, a feeling that given any fair chance to undertake dialogue with our opponents, we would be able to impress them with the basic rightness of our position. Unfortunately, by this approach alone we will not prevail because most people operate not rationally, but emotionally, on questions of sex in general, and homosexuality in particular.

"It is thus necessary for us to adopt a strongly positive approach, a militant one. It is for us to take the initiative—the offensive, not the defensive—in matters affecting us. It is time that we begin to move from endless talk (directed in the last analysis by us to ourselves) to firm, vigorous action.

"We *are* right; those who oppose us are both factually and morally wrong. We are the true authorities on homosexuality, whether we are accepted as such or not. We must demand our rights, boldly, not beg cringingly for mere privileges, and not be satisfied with crumbs tossed to us.

"The question of homosexuality as a sickness is probably the most important single issue facing our movement today. There are some who say that we will not be accepted as authorities, regardless of what evidence we present, and therefore we must take no positions on this matter but must wait for the accepted authorities to come around to our position—if they do. This makes us a mere passive battlefield across which conflicting 'authorities' fight their intellectual battles. I, for one, am not prepared to let others dispose of me as they see fit. I intend to play an active role in the determination of my own fate."

At a later date, Kameny further declared, "We've been shoved around for three thousand years, and we're tired of it. We're starting to shove back. And we're going to keep shoving back until we are guaranteed our rights! I say it is time to open the closet door and let in the fresh air and the sunshine . . . it is time to hold up your heads and look the world squarely in the eye as the homosexuals that you are . . . confident in the knowledge that as objects of prejudice and victims of discrimination you are right and they are wrong!"

Those were revolutionary statements.

In the years to follow, psychiatrists would eventually begin to examine the real gay world—and finally turn away from a labyrinth of sexual misconceptions that had been handed down to them from one charlatan after another since the Inquisition, when "put another faggot on the fire" was an instruction with more than a single meaning.

A new era was dawning, and by the mid-Sixties the sun was on the horizon. Eventually, history would prove that Franklin Kameny, Barbara Gittings, Kay Lahusen, and their friends were correct in the belief that the destiny of gay people would best be controlled by their own hands.

Gittings recalled, "Our thinking was beginning to become clear for many of us who were gay. At last, *we* were the experts on homosexuality—*not* outsiders with their financial or fanatical motives. During my first decade in the gay movement, on impulse I had accomplished things that seemed useful because they would have positive and immediate results. But I had only an undefined sense of mission, a mishmash of ideas about what could be achieved. Frank Kameny changed all that for me. He had fashioned a clearly focused philosophy for which I was searching. Nevertheless, there were countless homosexuals in whom repression was so ingrained that they were psychologically unable to push for their own emancipation. They defended their conviction by saying in effect, 'We have to leave the sickness question to the psychiatrists, and leave sexual research to the people whose business it is to come up with statistics and theories about us—they are the ones who must talk to the public in our behalf.'"

"Balderdash!" said Frank—and Barbara agreed.

With the new, more assertive agenda, Barbara soon found herself increasingly at odds with officers of the Daughters of Bilitis, and eventually there was mutual agreement that Barbara had more than fulfilled her "temporary" editorship of *The Ladder.* After three and a half years she turned the work over to another editor and pursued her new, equally challenging course, often working with Frank Kameny as he fought the United States Government in matters of security clearances and loss of employment for members of the gay community.

For gay men or lesbians in trouble, Frank and Barbara had explicit recommendations that boiled down to four vital points: (1) say absolutely nothing, (2) sign nothing, (3) get counsel, and (4) fight back! Frank declared, "It is the patriotic duty of every citizen to resist investigations and interrogations of homosexuals. Questions about homosexuals or homosexuality are never the proper concern of the government, and should not be answered."

Cases involving security clearances were often conducted in the Pentagon. Barbara, Frank, and whoever they were advising, would go to the meetings dressed very conservatively. "I wore a dress, and heels and hose," said Barbara, "and Frank always had on a suit, white shirt, and tie. We looked great, but there was one jarring note we employed to unsettle the hearing examiners. We wore one or two slogan buttons with blatant messages that were completely out of step with the rest of our conventional attire. The little buttons made statements like 'Cheers for Queers,' 'Gay is Good,' and one of the most deliberate eyepoppers of all time, 'Pray for Sodomy!'

"Publicity was the objective. So we held press conferences for the benefit of sharp-eyed reporters. And, when we first went into a hearing room, we made certain to shake hands with all adversary participants so those persons could not avoid reading our buttons. Throughout the rest of the day they had to either look at us or consciously ignore us, but they wouldn't be able to forget what our buttons said.

"As I grew older," admitted Barbara, "I found I cared less about what people thought. When the first invitations came to go on radio, I was scared, but I accepted. As it turned out, I enjoyed it. I was always ready to do something different, and I haven't had any regrets.

"Good times were part of the early years, even though you never knew what was going to happen. This was particularly true of some of the first gay conferences: How were hotel people going to treat you? Were they going to give you a hassle? Was there going to be a disruption from outside? Would police arrive and trump up some kind of stupid charge against us? All those things happened on occasion.

"But we had to take the chance. That's how I always felt. Every time I had to make a decision to put myself forward or stay back, to use my real name or not, to go on television or decline, to get out on some of the earliest picket lines or remain behind, I usually took the public position because there weren't many of us yet that could afford the risk.

"There were always unexpected jolts, some of them pleasant. When I agreed to appear on the nationally televised David Susskind show in 1971, I knew that I had to reveal my lifestyle to my mother. I couldn't just let somebody call her on the telephone and say, 'Have you seen your daughter—the lesbian!—on television?' So my mother was told in advance, although she was not comfortable with the information. The jolt came years later when she surprised me by revealing that following the Susskind program, a friend of hers had indeed called—to make negative comments about my being on the show.

"'At least Barbara's doing something to help others!' she replied.

"My lover was present as Mother related the incident. 'Did that "friend" ever raise the subject again?' asked Kay.

"'She did not!' said my mother."

As a counterreaction to the multipurpose hodgepodge of left-leaning gay liberation organizations that sprang up after the Stonewall Rebellion in 1969, the Gay Activists Alliance organized in New York City to concern itself specifically with only gay issues. Kay Lahusen was one of a small group of cofounders.

"Kay and I are considered mavericks within our movement," explained Barbara, "because we don't always agree with some of the other women's views on sexism and the use of language. But Kay was a cofounder of the Gay Activists Alliance because we were fed up with leftist shenanigans and a waste of our time by the Gay Liberation Front. The GLF had used our people as troops in a whole range of causes. We were marched to free prisoners at the Women's House of Detention. We were marched somewhere else to support the Black Panthers. Meanwhile, so little was being done for our own cause.

"A group in the GLF, we thought, was coopting our people for its own agenda, and although many gay people were unhappy about that, there was not yet an alternative. When Kay and others got together, they said, 'Let's have an organization devoted to gay issues only.' That's how the Gay Activists Alliance of New York came to be founded.

"The GAA was also firm in its belief that although it's very nice to get support from existing groups, it was an error to depend upon others. When the crunch comes," said Barbara, "outside associations will always use their money and energy for pressing needs of their own. Issues of gay employment, antigay church attitudes, homosexual parents, and so on, have to be dealt with by gay people. Groups like NOW and the NAACP will sometimes give us friendly assistance, but I would never expect organizations with nongay priorities to be a major resource in the gay rights battle.

"I want to deal with gay issues—first and foremost! For that reason, the National Organization for Women obviously was not for me. I have more in common with homosexual men than with heterosexual women. The last place I want to be in is a room filled with women talking about their babies. Child care is important, but let somebody else worry about it. There are millions of heterosexual women who can be tapped to fight for those concerns. But there aren't that many homosexual women and men willing and able to be upfront in our battle for gay rights.

"Gay organizations that spend an enormous amount of

time trying to deal with all the world's problems—not just homophobia, but racism, sexism, and other isms—mostly fall on their faces. As a matter of political practicality, the more issues a group adopts, the greater becomes the chance it will alienate prospective members." Barbara Gittings could never be accused of making such a mistake.

One organization that caught Barbara's attention combined two very special interests. Not only was this gay group strictly interested in the homosexual cause, it was also concerned with one of the major loves of Barbara's life—good gay books. Near the end of 1970, when Gittings was doing a weekly radio program, "Homosexual News and Reviews," on WBAI (the public station in Manhattan), she discovered in the program mailbox a notice that gay librarians had recently formed their own caucus in the American Library Association and were planning to promote gay issues and gay literature therein.

"Bells rang for me!" declared Barbara. "It seemed absolutely wonderful, and I had a sudden urge to be a part of that group. I knew the power of books. I could never forget how the heroines of novels had taught me something of gay life, how they helped me in a quest to find my people, and instilled in me the idea that we, as homosexuals, deserve the same opportunities as everybody else for the pursuit of happiness. Therefore, since the notice didn't say the new organization was for librarians only, I went to their next meeting. It turned out to be a very small gay group gathering in somebody's New York apartment, and they welcomed newcomers who could help, librarians or not."

Librarians are supposed to love lists, and this gay library group was no exception. They were planning a massive bibliography—a comprehensive list of everything in fact or fiction, pro or con, ever written or translated into English on the subject of homosexuality. In the meantime, however, a more modest short list of essentially progay materials (of which there was precious little in 1970) was needed quickly for an upcoming interim conference of the American Library Association.

"I found that I knew more about the existing gay literature than anyone else in the room," says Barbara, "so I was given the task of creating the list, which, in effect, became the first edition of our Gay Bibliography. I put together twenty book titles, plus notation of a dozen pamphlets and six articles, and printed the information on both sides of a single sheet of paper. Two thousand copies were handed out at the American Library Association's Los Angeles meeting in January of 1971. And the bibliography grew from there."

When Barbara's book list was first revised and reprinted, "Gay is Good," a logo adopted in 1968 by a national convention of gay groups, was added at the head of the page, and continued to be used for some years. Also, by happy coincidence, at the same time the bibliography's distribution began, the publishing industry realized that a market existed for gay subjects by gay authors. As a result, the first major tide of books by homosexual authors began coming through the publishing pipeline in the early 1970s.

"We were riding high along with the publishing industry, and it all worked very well," recalled Barbara, "because we got some extraordinarily good books at the time, some of which are still classics.

"I attended the large annual conference of the American Library Association held in Dallas, Texas, in June of 1971. Only a handful of us were present—as the Task Force on Gay Liberation—but we had energy beyond belief. One of the important objectives was to make ourselves seen.

"We presented two lectures. One was entitled 'Sex and the Single Cataloguer: New Thoughts on Some Unthinkable Subjects'—about prejudices reflected in library catalogues of gay information. The other was a talk by a gay man who had lost his job as a librarian solely because he was gay. Also, we aggressively distributed the 2nd edition of the Gay Bibliography. And we awarded our first Gay Book Award. Nevertheless, we might just as well have been invisible. Homosexuality was never more taboo. Try as we did, librarians at the conference scarcely took notice of our library-related, professional activities. Having a good message was no consolation if few would listen. So we knew we had to do something exotic to get their attention."

Thus was born the Kissing Booth, which, in its day, was infamous in Dallas!

"We were required to staff a booth in the exhibit hall for two hours on a sultry afternoon in the middle of the library conference. All that was expected from us was a dull display consisting of dust jackets from gay books, with our bibliography for a handout. It would have been very respectable and nice. And we could have been ignored some more. Instead, we decided to show gay love—live!

"Our exhibit was defined by plain gray curtains at the back and sides. At one end we put up a notice that proclaimed 'Women Only,' and at the other end 'Men Only.' In the middle of the booth, a cardboard strip proclaimed 'Hug a Homosexual.' I was with an attractive woman at one end, and the male founder of the task force was with a man at the other end. The four of us took our stations, and waited to dispense free same-sex kisses and hugs.

"We were calling, encouraging people to come over. Let me tell you, the aisles were jammed, but no one came into the booth. Everybody wanted to watch the action, but nobody wanted to be part of it.

"A *Life* photographer was there, and two Dallas TV stations were taking pictures, because it was the best news opportunity they'd had all week. A gay kissing booth? Hug a homosexual? In Dallas? Unbelievable!

"We put on a performance. With no takers from the goggle-eyed crowd, we kissed and hugged each other, called out encouragement, handed out our bibliography—and kissed and hugged each other some more.

"Dallas television featured the Kissing Booth on the news twice that evening and again the following morning. The library press wrote about us for the next six months. That stunt put our group on the map as far as the American Library Association was concerned."

Barbara became coordinator of the small gay task force within the Association, and continued in that post for fifteen years. Although the working membership of the national group rarely exceeded a dozen persons, that handful of people has made a tremendous behind-the-scenes impact. The fact that they have made gay reading lists widely available means that librarians, be they homosexual or otherwise, are able to offer important gay information to their clients, the readers, without any personal fear of being labeled as to their own sexual orientation.

The task force, unfortunately, does not work directly with libraries. In 1979, however, it did produce a booklet, *How to Get Gay Materials into Libraries,* which tells people what they, as individuals or as groups, can do to increase the availability of better, more accurate literature on homosexual subjects. The man or woman with a library card usually has as much clout in his or her own library as anybody else.

"I've always tried to promote books that favor our viewpoints," said Barbara. "From the very first we made a conscious decision to ignore the antigay material. Leave that to other list-makers. There are plenty of them with the time and the money. It's not of interest to us. We want to promote gay material that makes us feel better about ourselves and advances the cause. I think we've had enormous success.

"At Northwestern University I had failed classes while searching Chicago's libraries, nearly in vain, for intelligent information that I desperately needed in order to understand my life. A few years ago I returned to Northwestern for a speaking engagement, and a librarian came up to me after my speech and told me, 'You know, we automatically buy everything you recommend in the Gay Bibliography.'

"What a thrill it was—twenty years later—to be told that! But I never forget there are still a lot of scared gay people out there. Sometimes they call me by telephone. Mostly, they don't need professional counseling, just a few minutes' conversation with an ordinary run-of-the-mill gay person who can talk common sense to them, give a little advice, bolster their courage, and tell them their life can be marvelous.

"There are millions of homosexuals out there in the world who have no connection with the gay movement, who are running scared, wearing a mask. I met one while I was the invited gay speaker at a local divinity school that was having a conference on religion and homosexuality. When I was finished speaking, I remained to answer questions. The hostility in the room was palpable. The questions were harsh in the beginning, and got worse. I was holding my own, because over the years I've developed a tough hide. I can handle abuse if necessary. So I was fielding questions that were coming hot and heavy in my direction from those preachers-to-be when, without warning, a divinity student jumped up. 'Stop this!' he

protested. 'Stop attacking this woman! Because you invited her and you know who she is, you think she's the
only homosexual in this room. Well, you're wrong about
that! She's not the only homosexual here! I've lived with
you, and I've worked with you, and I've prayed and stud-
ied with you for three years, but none of you know that
I'm a homosexual too!'

"You could have heard a pin drop in that room. That
young divinity student was so upset about how I was
treated. I was used to a hostile reaction, but he wasn't. He
told me afterward that he never expected to do what he
did. He was simply galvanized into action. And it really
changed the whole atmosphere. That took a lot of courage.
It shook up the divinity school, and it shook up his career.
He wound up doing something else. Some years later he
told me that he never regretted blowing his cover.

"Nowadays there's a change in public awareness.
Nearly everybody concedes that he or she knows somebody, a man or woman, who's gay. That's important, because there's nothing that overcomes prejudice faster
than learning someone you're close to, or admire, is homosexual. It forces people to reevaluate their thinking.

"If every gay person came out, that might, by sheer
numbers, instantly end discrimination. But in the meantime, those of us who are visible have to concern ourselves with establishing gay rights in law. I hope the time
will come when none of us will need to hide anymore,
that eventually we can be treated as individuals, on our
own merits.

"It's not pleasant when you're dealing with nongay people, and you're on their wavelength with strong mutual
interests when, somehow, it becomes apparent you're gay.
Suddenly, an invisible wall goes up! You can feel the barrier! Things are never quite the same again. The relation-

ship changes because sexuality becomes the overriding issue, and all the good things that were going on before become incidental. That's something I would like to change. The problem is, a lot of heterosexuals can't make the leap beyond seeing us as homosexual, and therefore different.

"Remember the painted bird story? They took a bird from its flock and they painted it, then released it back among its own, and the flock pecked it to death. It was the same bird, but with slightly different plumage. The flock couldn't accept it. Yet it was their kind. There was nothing wrong with the bird. Sometimes I have a feeling, if we don't keep up our guard, they're going to peck us to death. Some are trying. It's wrong that we have to be afraid, but as vigilant defenders of our liberty, we must be ever watchful.

"I think one of the better aspects of our movement today is the mingling of men and women. My affinity has always been for all gay people on the basis of our common interest, not on the basis of gender.

"I grew up homosexual in a void, when there was virtually no literature. What did exist was most often dismally incorrect. There was little with which to identify. I had to find my own way, without any role models that I could talk to. I suffered a lot of anguish, alone, until a gay man befriended me.

"It's easier for young gay people today. They don't have to start from scratch to learn how to survive. The veil of silence has been lifted. It isn't necessary to be like people of my generation who grew up thinking, 'I'm the only one of this kind in the whole wide world!"

"There are still people hiding in the closet, fearful, trembling about what will happen to them if they're found out, or if they reveal themselves. But today's homosexuals don't start out thinking there is nobody else on earth like them, which was true of most gay people not too many years ago. At least now it's obvious they have plenty of good company. Our job in the movement, those of us who are already out, is to oil closet door hinges as fast as we can!

"Every group, big or little, in the gay movement that reaches out to involve gay individuals is engaged in important work. The beauty of our community is that we are doing a great variety of things. We have outdoors groups, athletes, naturalists, gay choruses and gay marching bands, political groups all along a full spectrum, groups in the professions and in business, campus groups, social groups, and hundreds of miscellaneous special-interest nooks and crannies. I'm delighted that as more and more gay people come along with their own varied interests, they are finding and filling the niches.

"Among the things that keep me going are the responses I receive. I owe a great debt to those gay people who've telephoned and written, telling me their stories that are sometimes sad, sometimes funny. The simple truth is, they are the people we do this for.

"Yes, I would like to change our world for the better, and I particularly don't want to see gay people growing up today and having to go through what I had to go through. I don't want to see an entire generation need to do it all over again. I want them to find themselves, and be at peace with themselves, and feel good about themselves.

"The gay community has put me in touch with proud and marvelous people. I know thousands who've come out, who've come into our movement—and the number keeps expanding."

Genesis

Harry Hay was a gay activist long before the word "gay" had its present meaning, or for that matter before the word "homosexual" was included in the average home dictionary. Yet, Harry, whose given name was Henry, is probably more responsible for the emergence of gay liberation and the degree of freedom gay men and lesbians in the United States now enjoy, than any other person who ever lived. Harry Hay was also an active member of the American Communist Party. How and why he became a member of the Communist Party, and what Harry brought from it, are vital to this story—which is, however, not a story of communism (for we are not authorities on the subject), but the story of a Communist who was a man of considerable courage.

He was conceived, Harry supposes, either in Scotland while his parents enjoyed their honeymoon among scenic highlands, or soon thereafter on the Gold Coast of Africa. Harry's father was an American mining engineer of Scotch ancestry, a self-made man, financially comfortable if not wealthy, and a Republican. When Harry was born, in 1912, Mr. Hay shared joint office space in London with another mining engineer, Herbert Hoover, who, sixteen years later, would become President of the United States. After leaving England, Mr. Hay managed Anaconda Copper's mining operations in Chile, then relocated to California.

For reasons of his own, Mr. Hay was never generous with his son. He gave Harry shelter, board, and clothing, which was no more nor less than his own father before him had provided; and he also saw to it that the boy was put to work at an early age.

While Harry was growing up in Los Angeles, every cent of spending money he had was money he earned himself. After school Harry delivered groceries on a bicycle. Saturdays, Christmas holidays, and half of every summer vacation he worked for a neighborhood store. Only the last precious weeks in August were Harry's—to camp at the north end of Catalina Island with a group of boys or to hike in the lovely but treacherous San Gabriel Mountains.

"I knew other kids had an allowance," admitted Harry, "but I never complained. No matter what you may feel, what can you do if your father is a Scotch autocrat and his word is law?"

In 1925, when Harry had just turned thirteen, it was decided by his parents that he should go to western Nevada for the summer. There he would labor in an uncle's hayfields. To the boy it did not matter that Mr. Hay had also been thirteen when first sent away. What did matter to Harry was that while he worked, his father would enable his mother, younger sister, and brother to take pleasant vacations and Harry was not invited. The all-too-evident discrimination would never be forgotten.

Long hours of pitching heavy bales of straw in the fields was hard work. At first, Harry thought he was going to die from the effort because, although he was a big kid, six feet tall and growing, the strength in his muscles had not caught up with his size. Fortunately, friendly, seasoned co-workers beside the boy cheerfully picked up the slack until, after a fortnight, he was finally able to more than hold his own. Harry's new friends, all older, provided a camaraderie and love of life that would remain in his heart forever. They were the Wobblies, an itinerant brotherhood of men who, in this instance, prospected or mined three seasons out of the year and came to the fields in summer.

Wobblies is a nickname of uncertain origin given to members of the Industrial Workers of the World, a labor organization founded in the United States. In their day, the Wobblies had tumultuous success, particularly in lumber, mining, and agricultural areas. Following World War I, the group steadily declined; but while the IWW thrived, it was good to its members, obtaining improved working conditions, including an eight-hour day, increased wages, and the luxury of riding the rails from one job to another without being harassed by railroad detectives. It was, therefore, with a genuine fondness for the IWW—plus some amusement—that the peripatetic Wobblies delighted in "educating" a boss's boy!

Harry worked with the Wobblies, slept where they slept, ate what they ate, and was making the same amount of money. On Saturday nights, when they went to the cribs and the speakeasies to spend the best part of a week's pay on prostitutes and bootleg booze, Harry accompanied them. Some of Harry's senior companions were of the opinion he should drink nothing more intoxicating than malt liquor at the bar, but Harry bought whiskey, in moderation, because he disliked beer. Nor did he enjoy the whores. After the boy had been encouraged to take his turn with one of the women clamoring for his virginity, he went to her featherbed, failed to appreciate the experience, and for many years thereafter avoided making a similar mistake.

Weeknights, which Harry preferred, he often read union tracts the Wobblies gave him, and on the following days, while pitching hay, Harry would be treated like a schoolboy, quizzed and tested by his friends. Soon he became knowledgeable about subjects of which his father would not have approved, including strike techniques and Marxist theory.

Harry learned about passive resistance, direct confrontation, and willingness to suffer physical injury or jail. He was impressed by stories of men and women who were trailblazers in the union's fight for free speech. Often, Harry was entertained with stories about an itinerant Wobbly named Joe Hill, who had written "Casey Jones" and a number of union songs. (Today Hill is best remembered because of Joan Baez' rendition of a popular folk tune, "I Dreamed I Saw Joe Hill Last Night.") As for Harry, he quickly absorbed the legend of a man who a decade earlier had created a furor of international proportions.

When Hill was arrested and accused of being one of two masked men who had assassinated a Salt Lake City grocer and his son, his many defenders claimed that the case against him was circumstantial, made only because of Hill's membership in the IWW. Conversely, anti-union spokespeople felt equally certain that Hill was "guilty as sin." The truth, unfortunately, will never be known. At the age of thirty-six, the condemned Wobbly was executed by a Utah firing squad.

The story of Joe Hill's martyrdom made a very strong emotional impression on young Harry; and, perhaps not coincidentally, he too would grow up and write words to be sung by people not content with the workings of society.

Harry Hay went to Stanford in California. College tuition and expenses were paid partly by a scholarship and partly by monies he had earned. There was no family contribution. Even if, quite out of character, his father had wanted to help, he could not. The year was 1930, the Great Depression was a reality, and Mr. Hay had lost everything in the stock market crash of 1929.

Harry found himself drawn to campus theatrical productions, where he had a degree of success. At the same time, certain that his collegiate charm depended greatly upon clever conversation and a good bedside manner, Harry instigated several sexual affairs, all very compelling, clandestine, and extremely confusing. The lovers were men, whom he actively sought and thoroughly enjoyed, but the moments of passion left Harry emotionally frustrated. When the urge for sex was drained, he pretended that women on campus were his focus of attention.

"I began to recognize my social life was getting impossibly confusing," Harry admitted. "Pretty soon I couldn't remember who I had told what. And I hate to lie. I hated to keep inventing stories in order to slip away to a speakeasy in San Francisco called Finnochio's, to art shows, the theater, and several blocks on Market Street where I could find men who pleased me. To avoid a continuing subterfuge, I decided to come out in my second year at college, admit openly to being 'temperamental' (a popular euphemism of the period), and find out what that would mean."

Harry's curiosity inspired what was, in 1931, an act of

folly. Students were carefully screened prior to acceptance. There had never been avowed homosexuals in the university. "And Stanford wouldn't have them!" an intramural coach declared, although he may not have been as naive as he pretended.

An eating group to which Harry belonged told him, "This might make things awkward for us socially. When anybody of importance visits, can you eat somewhere else?"

Some of Harry's classmates, including several who probably were also "temperamental," spoke more bluntly. "You'll understand if we keep our distance from now on?" one of them said. "We can't risk being seen with a queer!"

"They cut me dead," sighed Harry. "They never had anything more to do with me. Maybe I should have realized that would be their reaction—but I didn't."

Harry Hay was unable to finish school. His reasons included sinusitis and financial problems. As a cure for both, Harry returned to hay country, where work in a dry climate was good for him. Then, seven months later, at the urging of his mother (who knew he had done well on the Main Stage at Stanford) Harry went to the Hollywood Repertory Theater on Vine Street, determined to audition.

Five hundred hopeful actors answered the call, but Harry, who arrived at nine in the morning and waited until mid-afternoon to read, was hired. He was engaged to be the male understudy, which meant—since there were eight other men in the company—he had to learn numerous roles. For months he was busy. However, in the spring, there was time on Harry's hands—and he went seeking adventure.

One day, Harry heard there was going to be a mass protest in front of Los Angeles' City Hall, then under construction. Harry decided to attend. It turned out to be a demonstration with thousands of women asking that surplus milk, instead of being dumped into Long Beach Harbor, be given to mothers and babies. (Dumping to maintain milk's inflated price was an immoral act in the minds of those who were hungry—and many were hungry in 1933.)

Expecting to observe trade union activity, Harry was nevertheless caught up by the emotional outcry of desperate people. Soon he became involved in the heat of action. When several policemen on horseback plowed into the crowd, so closely packed together they could not move out of the way, Harry knew from what his Wobblies had taught him that the police were intentionally creating churning, pell-mell confusion. The resulting chaos would offer an excuse to call out the National Guard who, with rifles, were prepared to beat frustrated protesters out of the square and into submission.

Harry became livid watching the high-riding officers urge their horses into throngs of screaming humanity. Terrified women on either side were indiscriminately beaten with nightsticks. As the melee worsened, dozens were falling. Children and adults were in danger of being trampled. And Harry, overwhelmed by fury, suddenly could tolerate no more. He grasped a brick that was near, and without considering consequences hurled his missile at the closest mounted policeman.

"I don't remember throwing the brick," Harry admitted later. "I was caught up in my anger. The next thing I saw was the surprised cop falling from his horse. I have to say it gave me a thrill.

"In another moment, the people nearby became aware

of men in uniform moving toward us. They were searching for me, looking everywhere, getting misdirections from the crowd. As the police came closer, I heard a man behind me shout, 'Quick, get this kid away from here!' Seconds later, I was being pulled backward by many hands, and physically hauled into an old store, where I was hustled up about three flights of narrow stairs. There I was pulled out a back window onto the hillside against which the building was constructed."

Several people acted as guides. They hurried Harry to a large shabby house near the top of the hill where a streetwise, red-haired transvestite called Clarabelle was "queen mother" to the neighborhood's homosexuals. Clarabelle would not automatically hide just *any* fugitive from the law, but he intuitively realized that Harry "belonged."

"Go downstairs to the bottom floor," said Clarabelle. "There's a room with the door open. You'll find rolls of carpet inside. Get out of sight and stay there 'til I tell you it's safe."

Harry looked around, slightly dazed.

"Naughty boy, do you understand?" impatiently snapped Clarabelle.

Harry nodded.

Three-quarters of an hour later, Clarabelle sent a young man named Ted down to the room where Harry was hiding. Ted brought coffee and cake for Harry. In a short time, the two discovered many things about each other they liked. When the coffee and cake were gone, they reclined in a private area behind some purple carpets and enjoyed each other's company. Their pleasure lasted long after Clarabelle knew it was safe for Harry to leave.

*   *   *

A recurring pattern in Harry's existence was to seek another person to share his life. One of his great attachments (a hectic relationship that would irrevocably set Harry's course for the remainder of his years) began several weeks before the afternoon affair at Clarabelle's.

The revival of a pre–Civil War, hiss-the-villain melodrama that had successfully played on Broadway came to be staged in Hollywood—with Harry cast in many small parts. It was called *Ticket of Leave Man,* and told the story of an exiled convict who returns to England after many years in Australia. The outdated play, dripping with an excess of moral virtue, was played as comedy. In the title role was Will Geer, a stage actor. Will Geer looked like a lanky Tennessee mountaineer (and forty years later, he would become famous on television portraying the beloved Grandpa Walton). As the Ticket of Leave Man, Geer was hilariously funny—but Harry did more than laugh. Harry was enamored, and constantly alert for any opportunity to pause in the wings and stare at the star.

"Will's performances, the way he did things, were wonderful," Harry remembers with a smile and a faraway look. "In a way, Will was sort of ugly, the sort of ugliness that makes a man sexually attractive. That's how I felt. I was in love, and it was mutual. Our attraction to each other was intense for the better part of a year—and there was more to it than merely acting and going to bed.

"Will had been involved with New York theaters as a political organizer, and here in Los Angeles, Will recruited me. At first I didn't understand exactly what was happening. We went to a number of meetings. A lot of people talked with me. They looked me over, and I looked them over. Eventually, Will told me they were Reds. Then I had to decide whether or not I wanted to continue. Since anything Will Geer did was alright where I was concerned, there was never a question of turning away.

"I soon discovered membership in the Communist Party is not easy. They are very careful. Discipline is strict. And they want to be certain you have the courage to never betray anyone. Security was the reason none of us carried identification cards (which may come as a surprise to people who really don't know any better).

"Protection of others, not of one's self, was always a primary consideration. We didn't have personal telephone directories. Phone numbers were kept in our heads. It was an extremely rare occasion when photographs were taken. Private items were hidden. Nobody could trace anybody from anybody.

"One of Will's jobs was organizing a local Newspaper Guild. He also worked on the waterfront. And we were beginning to protest what was happening in Nazi Germany. There were mass turnouts for almost any excuse: International Men's Day, International Women's Day, This Day, That Day, Et Cetera Day.

"Sometimes we got arrested. I guess I went to jail about thirty times. In the lockup we expected to be knocked around by the police or beaten, and rarely were disappointed. That's something newspapers never reported. Most new members abandoned the scene after several arrests, but me, little by little, I began to like what I was doing. I liked the excitement of mass meetings and picket lines. I particularly liked the people.

"In 1934, hundreds of thousands of people were unemployed in the State of California. Many times more in the nation. Men, women, and children needed food, shelter, and clothing. They were nameless ciphers to big business. Elected officials favored the status quo. So we took every opportunity to tell the suffering about setting up cadres who could get them relief. To hungry people who had struggled all of their lives, we talked mostly about their right to have food, social security, pride, and a measure of self-respect. Can you imagine what it meant in those terrible times—to have any rights—even just one? Today, after half a century, whenever I remember the look on those faces I start breaking down in tears. To feel the joy that hope brought into their hearts, to have been a part of it, is something I can't forget!"

The Great Depression of the Thirties was ended by a major upheaval called World War II. On December 7, 1941, the Japanese, without a declaration of war, attacked Pearl Harbor early on a Sunday morning and killed many Americans. Germany was already mercilessly bombing London. Soon a long list of nations were involved in combat. American capitalists and Russian Communists became partners for the duration of hostilities. But in 1945, even as the Allies' victory drew near, relations between the Soviet Union and the United States turned cold, and the two superpowers locked horns in many arenas.

American Communists, including a majority who had been genuinely patriotic during the war, were suddenly denounced as spies. They went to bed friends and woke up traitors. High priest of the hysteria was a disturbing political opportunist, U.S. Senator Joseph McCarthy. Trampling civil liberties in the name of security, McCarthy temporarily deluded our nation into forgetting that subversion and the freedom to dissent are *not* one and the same.

Senator McCarthy really had only one objective, his own political power. In order to attain that end he found it expedient to attack "Commies under every rock," as one of his aides declared, and also, as an expedient afterthought, to expose "subversive, homosexual queers." The two separate groups never were related, but by 1947 it was common knowledge that a lot of gay men were being kicked out of the State Department. The reason given was that they were security risks, open to blackmail, but nobody ever bothered to learn if such allegations were generally valid (they were not). Loyal and dedicated homosexuals were dismissed in unjustified disgrace the moment their sexuality was discovered.

As McCarthy's network of informers and lawyers continued to hunt "Commies and queers," Communists, who had always been organized, went underground; and homosexuals, who had never been organized—and never expected to be organized—did their best on an individual basis to keep out of sight. The end result was that McCarthy's quarry was not defeated; it simply became more difficult to locate.

Harry Hay settled into being a political teacher, and an author of union songs consisting of his new words set to traditional music. He and some close friends were interested in the quality of life in their own diverse community. They worked against Jim Crow (antiblack discrimination), against restrictive covenants (housing discrimination), and against antisemitism. For the record, they also led fights for the advancement of working-class ideas, unemployment insurance, and other benefits sought by left-progressive unions.

"To be told by other Americans that we were captives of a foreign power was ridiculous!" exclaimed Harry. "McCarthy built up the Red scare, and then all important things we had done were viewed with suspicion. Anything having to do with the NAACP, the ACLU, and CIO, or employment of blacks, equality in trade unions, and whatever else the bosses opposed was under attack. We wanted to defend our side of the story, but were put down every time we tried."

The late 1940s were the beginning of a period when many Communists severed all relations with the Communist party, an organization that once may have numbered half a million American members. Harry Hay's active participation simultaneously declined. What happened in the next few months and years is the part of Harry's story that is of memorable importance to gay men and lesbians. It began when Harry turned his interest toward national politics.

Henry Wallace was a Presidential candidate and standard-bearer for the Independent Party. To qualify for California's primary elections, it was necessary that fifty responsible citizens of the state certify his name for the ballot. Included in the delegation was Harry Hay, and on August 10, 1948, he participated in the process with effervescent enthusiasm.

Harry's pleasure lasted all day. It had not lessened by evening when he attended a private beer bust. Close to the campus of the University of Southern California, the drinking party consisted almost entirely of gay theology students—a total of eleven. The number made a deep impression on Harry because it was rare for so many homosexuals to gather into a discrete and identifiable group! (In 1948, the practice of homosexuality was no less illegal than communism, and a simple arrest of gay men or lesbians was sometimes sufficient to precipitate unreasonable mental and physical abuse, including beatings and death from police and jailers.)

Danger notwithstanding, the imbibing students were not to be deterred; and before too many beers had been downed, amid laughter and story-telling, Harry turned the conversation to gay politics—an abstract idea that had not previously existed. It was an invented concept, to which no one would probably have paid any attention, even in jest, had not alcohol been amply available. The students all knew the Independent Party would have its convention in several weeks and, with Harry's encouragement, were soon saying, "Wouldn't it be wonderful if we could have a plank in Henry Wallace's platform, a statement that would speak for our own particular interests?"

After more beers, Harry suggested they band together under the name "Bachelors for Wallace." Several thought it would be a good idea if the Independent Party officially recognized the illegality of sexual entrapment, a national problem for gay men. Others wanted to eliminate antihomosexual discrimination documented in the recently published *Kinsey Report* on male sexuality. The conversation shifted to other subjects, but time and again returned to what seemed a quixotic idea, the possibility of gay pressure in politics.

At one o'clock in the morning when the festivities ended, Harry went home. He lay in bed, thinking, unable to sleep. Exciting ideas were springing to life in his brain. Moving to his desk, he began to work, writing quickly at first, then rewriting. He put on paper all the details required to make "Bachelors for Wallace" a reality. Soon he had several pages specifying how the idea could be implemented, how secret gay groups could be formed, and what their principles should be.

Harry knew what he was doing, drawing upon organizational knowledge he absorbed while working in the Communist Party. When Harry was finished, he had written not only a plank for the Independent Party's platform, but he had also outlined on paper a unit capable of implementing gay objectives after the election was over. Much of the work he proposed would include rudimentary efforts toward raising the consciousness of the majority of American homosexuals, who were still unaware of each other's existence.

Of primary importance was the need for a way by which ideas could be disseminated. The word "homosexual" was taboo in *The Los Angeles Times,* and many years would pass before any constructive news about gays or lesbians would even be mentioned in newspapers or on the radio. Therefore, communication would have to be person-to-person—or in forums that could reach out not only to gay individuals but also to friendly, socially conscious groups if any could be located.

Harry typed stencils, ran off two dozen copies on Ditto, and contacted his host of the night before. He obtained the names and telephone numbers of several of the theological students who, at the beer party, had seemed most interested in politics.

"You'll never guess," Harry said. "I went home last night and couldn't sleep, so I not only put down the points we talked about, I also worked out a plank for the platform. And I've planned for a group that can carry it out."

But responses were not like anything Harry expected!

"What are you talking about?" growled an about-to-graduate theologian.

"You know, our own plank in Wallace's platform," Harry explained. "Like what we discussed last night."

It was all to no avail.

The last man Harry called responded with a nervous laugh. "Oh, that was the beer talking!" he said. "You must know we're going into the ministry. You didn't really believe, did you, that we could be involved in anything so radical?"

Harry paused before answering. "Actually, I did," was his reply.

Disappointment was a part of the times, a part of the environment against which Harry Hay was willing to struggle. After living openly as a gay man in the early part of his life, and having personal knowledge of what it feels like to be discriminated against, he decided, "I'm going to do whatever I can to end oppression against minorities. I will dedicate my life, and one fine day in the future I might figure out how to work for the most discriminated-against minority of all—homosexuals!

"That was my earliest vision, and that is the reason I was involved in social reform through all of the Thirties. I always did whatever I possibly could, thinking I might stumble upon some answers and find a way gay people, my own people, might escape the clutches of bigotry and become first-class citizens. It was only imagination, but in my head it didn't seem completely unreasonable."

Harry pursued his dream. "We are a genuine minority here in the United States," he told those who would listen, "and as a legitimate minority we should be recognized. I know it's a brand-new concept, but the time has come to work for ourselves. As citizens, our concerns should be discussed. But we need to do some educating, starting with us. Most people really don't know what a homosexual is!"

Even with that provocative argument, Harry made little progress. If any gay men or lesbians agreed with Harry, they were afraid, and professional people were always extremely careful not to jeopardize their vocations. "Paranoia" became an overused word in decades to follow—but paranoia was already real in the Fifties, and for good reason. Harry worked to alleviate the fear.

"It was my idea to hold semipublic discussion groups," he explained. "Semipublic meant we would bring people together by invitation only, avoiding invading provocateurs who would be happy to tear us apart. At first, I wanted to have a responsible sponsor to act as the facade which would shield us from exposure, but even with interminable delays we were never able to have a homosexual group and a reliable sponsor interested at the same time."

Two years of frustration passed, years in which Harry sometimes amused himself with one of his earlier ideas. "I was not long out of college," Harry remembered, "when I thought it would be good for gay people if we lived in retreats of our own. I had in mind a little cattle ranch my grandfather owned in the mountains between Salinas and Fresno, completely isolated, where we could have a small, self-supporting community with only homosexual residents. I had nothing as elaborate as West Hollywood or San Francisco or Greenwich Village in mind. Who knew there were so many gays in the world? In those days it was difficult to think of our people in numbers exceeding several thousand. It was impossible to comprehend anything, yet, like twenty to thirty million!"

For a living, Harry worked as a production engineer in a boiler factory. Away from the job he was part of a group called "People's Songs." "Our group included Pete Seeger of the Weavers and Woodie Guthrie as our New York counterparts," he said. "We would take old folk tunes and give new words to the music for use on union picket lines or during protest demonstrations."

At CIO headquarters in Los Angeles, Harry was asked to teach folk music and its history. The course was popular, and by 1950, Harry was instructing several sections on various levels of accomplishment. Then Harry fell in love—again. And, partly to capture and maintain the new love's interest, Harry purposely revitalized his own recurring dream of gay unity.

Harry's new lover was a dancer named Rudi Gernreich, a Jewish-Austrian refugee (destined to become one of America's great fashion designers). In the beginning, as was not uncommon with Harry, he felt "electricity" drawing them toward each other. What followed may well have made theirs the most important affair in homosexual history. Endeavoring to avoid an early short circuit in the blossoming romance, Harry sought to sustain their relationship with a shared project. The result was that his physical passion rekindled his political passion. Harry took the gay-oriented papers he had written during Henry Wallace's campaign, updated and polished the ideas, improved structure, and presented all of his work to Rudi, from whom he desired approval.

Early the following day, Gernreich telephoned Harry at the boiler factory. "This is a wonderful idea you have," said Rudi, "but it reminds me of dangerous things I knew about in Germany. When Hitler took over, Jews were forced to wear the Star of David sewn on their clothing, and homosexuals were forced to wear a pink triangle. Those symbols led to concentration camps—and death! So careful—please! These meetings you plan must be very illegal. What will happen if United States Government finds out and come down on you?"

Rudi's challenge, or so it seemed, was like music to Harry's ears. Was there anything the government—federal, state, or local—could do to him that was not already familiar?

"Most of us in the Thirties had the courage of our convictions," Harry told Rudi. "We were outlaws then, and have been, for quite some time. The difference between being a political outlaw and being a sexual outlaw isn't much—it's like changing hats."

Rudi groaned. "If the State Department finds out I'm gay, me and my whole family will be deported!"

"Are you afraid?" asked Harry.

"Yes," replied the young refugee, "but I help anyway."

They went to the beaches. Between Pacific Coast Highway and the surf were narrow stretches of sand where homosexuals felt it was safer than in Los Angeles to congregate and enjoy the sun. Long-established locations were Will Rogers Beach in Santa Monica and a beach south of what would become the movie colony in Malibu. There was little to tip off strangers that those particular areas were different. No sign proclaimed GAY BEACH HERE. Homosexuals sunbathed in close proximity to each other, but any idea of tolerance was pure illusion. When either Harry or Rudi made known their dual purposes—gathering signatures for the Stockholm Peace Initiative, and seeking people who would be interested in joining a gay discussion group—there were many who were brave enough to sign the highly controversial anti-war petition; but as far as supporting any meaningful gay organization, their answers were always unanimous. "It's too dangerous!" sun-bronzed Adonises declared.

The risk was not imaginary. Licensed bars that catered to suspected homosexuals, even those establishments paying police protection, were often raided and closed for invisible infractions. There was no safe place. If a man in Los Angeles was entrapped, he usually had little choice but to go to one of two expensive lawyers who specialized in such cases.

Toward the end of October 1950, Rudi told Harry with evident frustration, "We've been trying to get people interested in a group for three months. I've talked to everybody I know. Still we haven't come up with anybody to start this thing."

"I know," replied Harry.

"Well, we have to do something!" proclaimed Rudi. "You and I, the two of us, are not enough. What about in your folk music classes? You said some of them union guys might be gay."

"It is possible."

"So talk to those people! Have you ever showed them the call?"

"No, Rudi, what for? They don't have a nickel any more than we have. They can't help us. We can't afford to hire a hall. We can't even afford to send invitations."

Rudi let out a snort of annoyance. "Show it to them! We must start somewhere!" he said with impatience.

Therefore Harry made several new copies of his proposal and at the next opportunity nervously showed it to two men in his class he assumed were gay. (Harry knew they had lived together in the same house for a time and might have been lovers.) Chuck Rowland, in charge of production control at a furniture factory, had been a Communist organizer for American Youth for Democracy before World War II. Bob Hull was an accomplished pianist, but worked as an organic chemist. He had been a trade union organizer in Minneapolis. They were the next two people to endorse Harry's plan.

Saturday, November 11, 1950, was Armistice Day, and windy. Harry lived in the Silverlake area of Los Angeles. Shortly after nine in the morning, Chuck Rowland called and told Harry that he and Bob Hull would like to visit and bring a friend with them. The friend was Dale Jennings.

As soon as Harry finished speaking to Chuck, he made another telephone call. "Something seems to be happening, Rudi. I think you should be here," he told Gernreich.

"I remember Chuck coming up the driveway," Harry

said later. "He was waving the call I had given him two days earlier, and shouting to me over the breeze, 'I wish I had written it myself!' Chuck hollered. 'When do we get going?'

"Oh, it was a grand day!

"The five of us went out on the brow of the hill, overlooking the east side of the Silverlake Reservoir, and we began what would, with some difficulty, eventually become the Mattachine Society. What a moment! It was the first time five sincere people had ever gotten together as a gay political group. We found out about each other, and we talked about ideas. That's the way a community begins."

Their first semipublic discussion group was held on the fifteenth of December 1950. The meeting was at Otto K. Olsen's, an electrical contractor on Vine Street, who rented space. Of twenty persons invited, only four arrived, and even they had some fear. A month later, in January, four guests came to the second meeting, but they were not the same four as in December.

During the spring and summer of 1951, the Mattachine Society's existence became barely perceptible. Local homosexuals very slowly began to realize that some of their own were attending meetings—somewhere—but for almost all homosexuals, caution would continue to be the watchword. Often, when a curious gay man did venture into a Mattachine meeting, he would almost inevitably be accompanied by a woman (usually a lesbian friend) whom he would falsely introduce as "my wife" or "my girlfriend" or "my fiancée." Nobody admitted he or she was gay or lesbian!

In spite of all difficulties, the struggling Society slowly continued to grow. In a year, by the fall of 1951, discreet little meetings were being held in San Pedro, Wilmington, Long Beach, Whittier, Capistrano, San Diego, occasionally in Laguna, and three locations in Los Angeles. Soon there were too many groups for the founders to handle alone, and a few guilds were created to observe and direct discussions, which continued to be semipublic.

Each guild consisted of not more than ten men, and only one of those men had secret, memorized information making it possible to communicate with another guild. These extreme protective divisions of knowledge were derived from the structure of secret fraternal orders—precautions learned by Harry Hay during his Communist days in the political trenches.

It is reasonable to assume that the Mattachine Society, the first viable homosexual organization in America, could not have survived in the early 1950s without what may now seem like an excess of caution. Open-mindedness was not a popular commodity at the midpoint of the twentieth century. Mattachine telephones were tapped. Members were prevented from sending liberation literature through the United States mails. Every battle against oppression was booby-trapped with fear. And yet it was oppression in a particularly vicious form that propelled the determined Mattachine dream into a dynamic reality.

Dale Jennings, one of the five original members of the Society, was despondent, having recently severed his relationship with a lover; and in March of 1952, Dale moved to the Westlake area of Los Angeles near MacArthur Park. One dreary Saturday evening, he was alone, leaving a restroom near the lake, when a man approached and, without encouragement, began making sexual propositions. Disliking the fellow, and uncomfortable with the man's crude advances, Dale retreated. However, the unidentified individual, a persistent undercover LAPD vice officer, followed Dale from the park and eventually bluffed and bullied his way into Dale's nearby apartment. Once inside, he went to the living-room window and pulled down the shade, signaling a waiting policeman, who rushed upstairs.

"I didn't want anything to do with him!" Dale insisted when Harry posted his bail early the following morning. Dale was terrified, but at the same time, furious. "The bastard's story is all a fabrication!" he said as they walked from the warm jail into the cool dawn.

It was then they decided not to play the customary judicial game. They would go outside of the established system to fight the entrapment. It was the only way they might win. Instead of hiring one of the two smug attorneys who lunched with judges and victimized clients, they enlisted a very good "longshoreman's lawyer," George Shibley, who said, "Sure, I'll take the case, Harry. I owe you because you are one of the best Marxist teachers I ever had. You'll have to help me with this, though—I don't know a damn thing about homosexuality." But Shibley knew enough about oppression, and homosexuality was not a threat to him. He quickly understood Dale's situation.

The most pressing problem was to raise money for trial costs. With that objective, Harry, Dale, and other friends set up the "Los Angeles Citizens' Committee to Outlaw Entrapment," using the address of Harry's mother, who lived in Hollywood. Every weekend, Mattachine groups reproduced leaflets, which they handed to people outside of grocery stores, thumbtacked to telephone poles near bus stops, left on streetcar seats, and posted in libraries or any other place bulletin boards were available. Even gay decorator shops on Robertson Boulevard were enlisted to slip leaflets into the shopping bags of customers.

The leaflet made the point that because gay people go to certain places, their mere presence is insufficient reason to be arrested. Such a conclusion is guilt by association. Many gay people who saw the leaflets began to realize that a group in Los Angeles was *actually* fighting an entrapment case. Before, nobody had ever realized that a defense was possible!

Harry's mother began to receive telephone calls. Men and women went to her home and donated five dollars as they told their own sad stories. Fifteen hundred dollars were raised that way for Dale Jennings' trial. At Trancas, near Zuma Beach (north of Los Angeles), two hundred fifty people paid to attend a fund-raiser, and gays danced with each other and lesbians danced with each other in public! Invited onlookers were stunned. Late arrivals stopped in the doorway and stared. People were thrilled. Never in their lives had they ever seen so many homosexual people together. And not only were the people gay and lesbian—they were *openly* gay and lesbian—dancing with one another and having a good time.

"It was wonderful!" laughed Harry. "Being obvious in those days was unknown. Even in a bar one was never obvious. So the people arriving at Trancas couldn't believe their eyes. We took the opportunity to show them the call, letting them know we were loving people who loved being gay. It was something they had never heard. Being gay was supposed to be dirty! But we were something different. We stood for dignity and freedom, and it was very exciting!"

As the date for Jennings' trial neared, Harry sent daily press releases to every newspaper, radio station, television station, and all the even faintly liberal journals in America. Not a word was printed or spoken on the air. There was a total blackout—a conspiracy of homophobic silence. It was as if nothing was happening.

Nevertheless, George Shibley was magnificent in the courtroom. He managed to reveal jury tampering, and he proved one of the sworn vice officers was perjuring himself—lying from the witness stand. His summation held gay spectators spellbound. "Yes, my client is a homosexual," they heard Shibley say (and there were gasps from people listening). "My client is not only a homosexual," continued Jennings' defense, "he is also a decent, dignified man with great self-respect."

Nobody had ever heard anybody say something like that in court before. It was an important beginning. The result was a hung jury, and for obvious reasons, the city decided not to press charges again.

"We wrote a short victory statement and handed out twenty-five thousand copies all over town," exulted Harry. "After that we grew by leaps and bounds! It was the big breakthrough! We even got letters from foreign countries. In a letter that came from New South Wales in the fall of 1952, a man from so far away wrote, 'I know that there will never be such a thing as gay affirmation in my country in my lifetime, but I just wanted you guys in America to know that the word Mattachine spells hope along the wind.'

"Hope along the wind! A phrase I won't ever forget."

If Harry Hay had not worked with the Wobblies and embraced their fight for revolutionary beliefs, if he had not always been a lusty homosexual, if he had ever wavered in his resistance to the powerful and pervasive anti-gay establishment, it is probable there would never have been a Mattachine Society—an organization that in the darkest years of fear and repression gave birth to new generations of pride.

The mystery is gone, but it is moving to recall some

extremes of caution and discretion that the Mattachine Society realized were necessary in the process of embracing new members. At first, prospective members would be observed as guests attending semipublic group discussions. If the individual seemed interested, if his eyes opened at the "right" moment, the next time that person was in attendance, two members of the inner circle would observe him. If that hurdle was passed, the person might be asked to dinner and shown the Society's written statement of "Missions and Purposes." Assuming he could support those ideals, he would be invited to a meeting on a more advanced level of discussion, a meeting he never would have known about otherwise. There would be philosophical give-and-take, people sounding out each other, and eventually, if everyone felt comfortable, the newcomer would finally be welcomed into the inner circle.

"It was a special ceremony," Harry recalls with some emotion, his eyes moist in remembrance. "The new person would stand in the center of a circle as we spoke of our purpose and our commitments to one another. Then at a certain point, we would momentarily break the chain and rejoin with the new and precious link. Anybody who has ever been through that ceremony can never forget it.

"Our declaration always ended, 'We hereby resolve that the day will come when no young person shall ever step out into the dark, alone and afraid, again!'"

So the Mattachine Society began. And although the original association no longer exists except in memory, the heritage of that semipublic, semisecret company of dedicated men was the forerunner of all gay and lesbian organizations that now operate in the open and that are happy to forget that a few decades ago there was a social and political environment so hostile to homosexual existence that the bigotry of today pales by comparison.

A Gift
of Love

◥◣

Blessed with a talent for telling anecdotes, serious, comic, or satirical, Ivy Bottini developed a stand-up monologue derived from her own experiences, including every woman's frustration with society, discrimination in the workplace, and lesbian problems in marriage. With her commentary, Ivy toured America. The forums into which she was booked often included colleges, and the expression of appreciation she most enjoyed was received from a rumpled professor of mathematics, who found Ivy backstage following an evening performance. "While I was listening to you," said the man, "I stopped laughing for a minute, and the truth of what you were saying dawned on me. I never knew until now why my wife divorced me!"

Dissolution of a marriage is difficult at best. The plight of parties concerned is compounded when the husband, or the wife, or both are not even aware of homosexual forces pulling their relationship apart. To be part of that not uncommon marital trauma, to endure, and to triumph, requires fortitude and the greatest personal courage. Ivy Bottini's own story includes many of these elements.

In 1926, Ivy was born in a house divided by three factors: alcohol, temper, and the town line. Straddling an invisible boundary, only the front of her home was in Malvern, Long Island. The back of the building was in Lynbrook, a small town with a single train track. Ivy and her playmates ran across the railroad ties every day. The children were never warned, and never realized, that exposed beneath a wooden strip parallel to the track's visible steel was an electrified third rail. It was survival, more than birth, that seemed to be a miracle.

Ivy's parents were Irish and English. Life at home was stormy. Dad drank "a little too much," and Mother had no patience. They made a handsome couple when there was calm, but all too often, screamed retorts were hurled in all directions. Ivy learned to get out of the way.

Her favorite classes were usually in a gymnasium. Like many girls her age, Ivy developed crushes on athletic instructors, and after secretly being in love with a succession of them, without understanding the attraction, there was little wonder that Ivy wanted to become a gym instructor herself. "Miss Rose and Miss Buck were wonderful teachers," remembers Ivy. "Miss Rose could whistle through her teeth, and Miss Buck joined the Coast Guard."

Ivy was accepted for admission to Pennsylvania State University, where she wanted to study physical education, but when her mother learned about the plan, entailing a move away from home, it fast became apparent to everybody within shouting range that the idea was anything but acceptable. "I guess I was my mother's safeguard," suggested Ivy, "because if I was present when she and my father started throwing things, they could count on me to step in the middle and prevent either one from hurting the other."

Miss Wilson taught typing and shorthand. "She was a saving force in my life, like a second mother," Ivy recalled with a smile. "I even got to call her Peg. In physical education and art, I was a straight-A student, and Miss Wilson really helped by encouraging me to continue studying the art. When I took my tough at-home drawing exam for Pratt Institute in Brooklyn (a short train ride from Long Island), I was invited to Peg's quiet apartment and worked at her kitchen table, sketching the intersection we could see from her second-story window.

"I really loved Peg, but we didn't talk about intimate things. In high school and even in college, I never spoke to anyone concerning my attraction toward women. Never a soul!"

Toward the end of Ivy's first year at Pratt Institute, an automobile accident took the life of her father, a Long Island cab driver. (The taxi he was driving was struck by a drunk driver.) Days later, Ivy was called into the main office at Pratt. "The directors and I are sorry to hear what happened," she was told by the dean of the Advertising Art Department. "We thought you and I should have a little chat about tuition. We'd like to know if you can afford to continue your studies?"

Ivy shook her head. She was aware that her finances were threadbare. There was already talk at home about having to withdraw from school. As a result, she was quite unprepared for the next words she heard.

"We'll help you," said the dean. "Pratt is offering a scholarship. All you have to do is accept."

Ivy wanted to cry.

The kindness was a complete surprise.

In the future, Ivy's creativity justified Pratt Institute's confidence. "After graduation, I made a good living with my artwork, and it was always very fulfilling," she declared. "I did fine art as well as commercial."

There were shows in galleries. An art critic wrote, "Ivy paints with the strength of a man." His statement prompted her to comment, "I disliked his statement, although I didn't analyze it at the time. I knew I didn't paint like a man. That wasn't what I was, and it wasn't what I had learned. I painted like me!"

In her spare time, Ivy's appreciation of competitive sports continued. Although her intermittent dream of becoming a university-trained athletic instructor never materialized, she did continue her association with females in sports—not only in school but for many years thereafter—spending a considerable amount of time coaching and playing on women's teams engaging in modified hardball, basketball, and hockey.

Meanwhile, after her father's death, an element of stability entered Ivy's life. She and her mother moved to live with her Aunt Edna and Uncle Phil on the opposite side of Lynbrook, near the East Rockaway line. Aunt Edna's home was different from the home Ivy's father had provided. The new environment was one of control rather than chaos, with everything in its proper place. No more was "Hey, anybody see the salt?" answered by "I think it was under the bread."

The road leading to one of Ivy's greatest adventures, a marriage of sunshine and shadows, began without her knowledge while she was still living in the home of her aunt and uncle. Across the street resided a shy, asthmatic young man, recently returned from military duty in World War II, who secretly watched from an upstairs window as the desirable young woman was going to school or returning. Not until a couple of years had passed did Ivy become more than peripherally aware of Eddie Bottini's existence.

They began to go out on double dates. Ivy never complained when, sometimes, the fellows sat in the front seat of an automobile and the young women sat together in back. Eventually, however, the day came when Ivy and Eddie decided it would be "nice" to be married. Ivy, who had been engaged on four previous occasions, and had a history of changing her mind when wedding bells and orange blossoms became too real, described the days immediately before their wedding.

"I was totally fear-ridden," she declared. "A week before the date set for the ceremony, I felt like I was waiting for my execution. I couldn't eat. My throat was constricted. I could chew, but I couldn't swallow.

"On a conscious level I kept asking myself why I always preferred going on double dates rather than just two of us being alone. And I was constantly questioning my own sincerity and wondering why I was different. That kind of dialogue was often batted back and forth inside of my head. I kept trying to believe my apprehension was merely a passing phase, but was terrified of the wedding, convinced I couldn't walk the length of the aisle. I was certain I wouldn't be able to speak.

"Our family doctor sent me to an analyst. When the analyst asked what my problem was, I said, 'I have such awful anxiety. I can't eat.' He peered into my eyes, and in desperation, I allowed a sense of trust to develop. When he asked what was really causing the bother, I blurted out words that were surprising, even to me. 'I think I love women!' I said.

"The analyst paused. I watched for his reaction while he watched for mine. 'Have you ever kissed—a girlfriend?' he asked.

"'No!' I answered without the slightest hesitation. The very idea was shocking. It had never occurred to me.

"'Then you are not a homosexual,' the analyst announced with what passed for certainty. 'Go ahead—be married—and get on with your life, but give up sports and make friends only with married women,' he said.

"It's difficult to describe the relief those words brought into my heart. Suffice to say that happy in my ignorance (and his), I responded, 'Oh, thank you, thank you—thank you!' If he'd put out a hand, I would have kneeled and kissed his ring. That was in 1952.

"Needless to say, I survived to be married. When the time arrived for the ring part of the ceremony, I was so excited that I held out the wrong hand. It was funny. Eddie slipped the gold wedding band on a wrong finger. For several weeks afterward, I was not absolutely convinced that our marriage was completely legal!"

The newlyweds moved to the most famous tract of mass-built single-family dwellings in America—Levittown, Long Island—where they bought a house and made it a home. "Eddie was a very nice guy," Ivy acknowledged. "He was easygoing. Probably the only man in the world I could have married. Eddie was also comfortable. I felt safe with him. The problem, eventually, would be me."

Ivy followed the analyst's advice by severing almost all association with the teams she had coached, although she continued to have dinner with a few of the women once or twice a year. Free time was rechanneled to socialize with married friends. It was an easy adjustment. Ivy merely shifted her affection from a few single women in New York to a few married women in Levittown. It was just as easy to have a crush on a neighborhood housewife over a morning cup of coffee as it was to adore the star basketball player in a gymnasium alive with shouts and echoes.

The Bottinis' first daughter, Laura, was born in 1953. Lisa arrived three years later. Ivy, who had always been accustomed to taking an active part in community affairs, merely added the joys of being a mother to other aspects of her life. In 1955, she went to work for *Newsday*, Long Island's extremely successful evening tabloid. After four years in advertising, she was promoted and became an editorial artist, designing the newspaper's feature pages and its monthly magazine.

"I wasn't the kind of woman who stayed put," said Ivy. "I worked the late-night shifts, leaving for the job about the time Eddie came home, then getting back to the house at one in the morning. I was a mother in the daytime. That's how I liked it."

The only problem was that in 1959 the workable, orderly world of the Bottinis slowly began to unwind. Ivy became pregnant for the third time—resulting in a psychological nightmare of extensive proportions. The baby died. Ivy also came very close to dying.

After the death of the baby, Ivy was confined to bed for seven torturous months with no responsibilities. Extended contemplation and endless hours without physical activity gave demons from the subconscious every opportunity to assault Ivy's brain with doubts and desire. Perspiration dampened the bedclothes as Ivy began examining feelings she had always considered taboo. "I've almost died in this bed that somebody else made," she kept repeating to herself, "and I haven't ever lived a life of my own. Somebody else has used this body, but it sure isn't me. I haven't even begun to know who I am. Somebody else has been trained to be mother and wife. That other person has lived, but their soul is not mine."

Ivy's personal dissatisfaction increased. She emerged

from the hospital totally depressed. Not only was losing the baby difficult to accept, but returning to work had no appeal. Living had become drudgery. The cheerful, energetic Ivy of the past was nowhere to be found.

"I can't function," she told her regular doctor.

"Your problem sounds more emotional than physical," he told her, and recommended a new psychiatrist. An appointment was made, and Ivy soon found herself speaking with another medical practitioner, urgently asking for help. As before, after only brief conversation Ivy was once again desperately blurting out words which in those days were inevitably self-damning. "Doctor, I think I love women," she heard herself say.

Later, Ivy recalled, "I couldn't believe I had blabbed it again. But pow! I did. And it released some of the pressure."

The revelation was less agreeable to the psychiatrist. "If you persist in this kind of thinking, you will harm your children," he said. "You don't want to hurt your children, do you?"

"No," replied Ivy.

"You love your children?"

"Yes."

"You really do care for your husband?"

"Yes."

"Then you will have to struggle with those feelings. We'll work on this without anybody else's knowledge until you're cured, and we'll see that you're readjusted back into marriage."

"Thank you, thank you!"

For the next few years, the psychiatrist repeatedly cajoled and deluded Mrs. Bottini into believing she was ill and that a cure existed. For months at a time Ivy would feel satisfied with her life and with society. Then something would happen to disturb the status quo, and she would hastily return to the expensive psychiatric therapy.

"But the process of readjusting to marriage was less and less satisfactory," said Ivy. "The reason therapy even helped at all was probably because I was never thinking physically about women. I didn't dream about sex or holding and kissing. It was just this wonderfully intimate sense of association I felt.

"Other parts of my life were my job at *Newsday*, my family, and local politics," said Ivy. "When the children were young, I was actively involved with their schools. There were battles on the school board, and I participated for a number of years. The ultra-right-wing John Birch Society wanted to do away with physical education, extracurricular activities of all kinds, even school lunches. Reading, 'riting, and 'rithmetic were about all they wanted. For my part, during the period when I considered them a threat, I was very active in organizing the community against the Birchers—and we defeated them."

When the women's movement blossomed in 1966, Ivy was still happily working for *Newsday*. Also working for the tabloid was an ace reporter named Dolores Alexander, for whom Ivy felt a particularly strong attraction. Early one October evening, the telephone in Ivy's art department rang. The caller was Dolores, who had just returned from an historic press conference held in Manhattan by a small but important group of ten or eleven women led by Betty Friedan, who had announced formation of the National Board of the National Organization for Women.

"Can you come into the city room?" asked Dolores, adding, "I want to give you something." Minutes later, Dolores handed a sheet of paper to Ivy. "Join this," said the reporter.

"What is it?" asked Ivy.

"Don't ask—join."

"Okay," said Ivy, reading rapidly.

She would have done many things, within reason, for Dolores. "Within the month," said Ivy, "I was a founding member of the National Organization for Women's first chapter, which was established in New York City. That meant spending a lot of time commuting into and out of Manhattan. I got to meet a wide variety of women—women who were often considerably different from my circle of friends in Levittown. This was an entirely different world, far removed from suburbia.

"Some of the women were married. A majority were single. Many were in professional fields. On some level of consciousness, I knew and was intrigued by the knowledge that in the group there had to be others like me, women who particularly liked the company of women. I later realized that numerous leadership positions in the early days were filled by closet lesbians, although the number of homosexual rank-and-file members were few (particularly when compared to what outsiders wanted to believe).

"It took courage to get involved with the women's movement in the Sixties. NOW was a very threatening concept to many, and not all of our enemies were men. NOW called into question not only who owns what in this world but also who owns whom. We were considered militant, radical, strange—because we were raising issues about the very foundations of society.

"Excitement grew in the women's movement because we believed in a vision of what could be accomplished. At the State of New York's Constitutional Convention, we argued in favor of what were called 'reproductive rights'—which were not narrowly defined as abortion rights. Reproductive rights," explained Ivy, "meant women are not chattel for others to control, but that we are free to decide for ourselves what is good, or not good, for our own individual bodies."

Another endeavor of the National Organization for Women was to "desexigrate" *The New York Times.* That effort took several years, but it was finally achieved. Today, the accomplishment is remembered only as a footnote in publishing history. The problem was that want ads always read "Men Wanted, "Women Wanted," or to a very limited degree "Men/Women Wanted." These classifications had the result that the majority of occupations were traditionally offered to only one gender or the other—with women more often than not the financial losers. To counteract the unsatisfactory situation, NOW picketed *The New York Times,* trashed its editorial offices by bringing in and depositing thousands of old copies of the newspaper tied up in red tape, and harassed the *Times'* publisher with telephone calls, letters, and sit-ins until the world's most prestigious daily capitulated to the women's demand for better and more equal hiring practices. Other newspapers immediately followed the leader.

Elected president of the New York Chapter of the National Organization for Women in 1968, Ivy was still holding that office when the first Women's Equality March on Fifth Avenue was planned. "It was fascinating," Ivy remembers. "I had no idea who would show up for the big parade. We were only certain of the participation of our own members, who were leading it off. After dispersing the last troops, I walked toward where the line of march was beginning. My greatest expectation was that we would have gathered a parade contingent of as many as four or five hundred persons—if all went as expected—and if our media promotion had been well-received by the public.

"As I looked around the corner, I literally gasped at the sight on Fifth Avenue. I saw nothing but humanity! One of the most thrilling moments of my life! There were thousands and thousands of advancing people, predominantly women. There were banners and posters of every color and description—a flood of determination! Many wonderful men joined with us. There were always some men in the group because we were the National Organization *for* Women, not the National Organization *of* Women."

Those were the good times—but dark storm clouds were massing on Ivy's horizon. As her involvement with the women's movement became stronger, Ivy became increasingly aware of a need to truthfully discover herself. She was still seeing her psychiatrist—with increasing frequency—and he was still adjusting her back into her marriage.

In the back of her mind Ivy had always entertained the vague probability that some of the women whom she had coached on basketball teams were lesbians, and partly for that reason she had maintained a tenuous contact. On a wintry afternoon, Ivy impulsively called one of the players and made a date. Later, when they sat in the friend's living room, Ivy confided, "I'm not certain, but I have this idea—I think it's possible I might be—don't laugh—a homosexual."

The athletic friend observed Ivy, at first with disbelief, then with a widening grin. "We thought you would never arrive!" she said.

"You knew?" asked Ivy.

"We all knew."

Ivy allowed her head to slump forward, astonishment turning into feigned annoyance. "In the many years we've known each other—why didn't you tell me?" she asked. Then she added with some exasperation, "If somebody had just told me—all the pieces of my life would have gone together and made some sense. But nobody ever said a word."

The friend laughed. "We didn't know you wanted to hear. But now, is there anything I can do to help?"

Ivy considered a moment, then answered, "Yes, I've heard about gay bars. Can we go to one? I've been curious."

"Follow me," said the friend.

The next few hours were a revelation. "I remember sitting at the bar watching women dancing with women, and men dancing with men," said Ivy. "I was fascinated. And I felt comfortable even though to me it was new. It was as though I'd finally come home.

"The next night was a Saturday, and I returned to the bar alone. On that occasion, I met Nancy, a bright, pretty woman who increased the rate of my pulse. Nancy was a good dancer, as was I. The music played. We spun around. And in my head there were radical thoughts of being able to live my own life. The feeling was extraordinary.

"Afterwards, I felt guilty, and soon decided it was probably best to avoid any more dancing for a time. However, as sincere as I was about discouraging my inner self, mother nature had different ideas!"

One severely cold morning several months later, when predawn darkness hid the snow-covered landscape, warring desires within Ivy's head met in furious confrontation. It was the inevitable moment when an anguished cry from the heart became so insistent that every inaccurate idea concerning sex that her family, church, and society had ever taught her was shattered into countless, unmendable pieces. The climactic turmoil was a dramatic extension of the night before.

Ivy had attended a NOW meeting until late in the evening, and instead of going home to Eddie, spent the night with her reporter friend Dolores. That relationship was never complicated. There were no mutual sexual overtones. "Between our involvement with NOW and our work at *Newsday*, Dolores and I spent a lot of time together," said Ivy. "That was great. I loved her so much, but I knew it was all there could be—and my frustration became increasingly intense.

"Evenings when I stayed over with Dolores, our usual practice was to share a bed, but I never allowed myself to think on a sexual level. The most that ever happened was that I might dare touch her hand when she was asleep, or very carefully place my foot alongside hers.

"After such a night of relentless temptation, with little if any sleep, I was returning to work, alone, remembering our closeness. As the train slashed through the dawn, racing from Manhattan to Long Island, my thoughts became more distorted with each rattle of the railroad cars, and devils of despair twisted whatever I was thinking. My personal dissatisfaction kept growing stronger until, at a moment when the train stopped for an intermediate station, I could no longer ignore my frantic emotions.

"I ran for the door just as the train's wheels were again beginning to turn, and frantically jumped out on the station platform. I needed to get away from colliding ideas. But I didn't know where I was, or where to go, or how to be free. I had only the overwhelming feeling that escape and sanity were linked together and had something to do with never going home again.

"I found a telephone and, with shaking fingers, despite the early morning hour, dialed the number of my sleeping psychiatrist. As his telephone rang, I realized a storm was blowing. Drifts of snow were forming against some buildings. Finally, the doctor answered. 'Where are you?' he asked with crushing displeasure.

"'Somewhere on the south shore of Long Island,' I told him, and then I said, 'I can't go home! It's wrong, Doctor. I know what you've said, but I just can't go back anymore!'

"'Why are you out at this ungodly hour?' he asked, after a pause.

"'I was going to work,' I answered, shivering in the penetrating cold, 'but I got off the train. Everything is crazy. I'm terribly confused. I don't know what I should do.'

"There was another pause. Then, obviously feeling very inconvenienced, the therapist said, 'Well, I can't see you at this hour. Call later, when the sun comes up.' Before I could protest, he hung up on me. That was the last time I ever spoke to him."

Abandoned, Ivy sought other assistance. Her decision was to contact Esther, a friend from her married group. When Esther answered the telephone, Ivy repeated the same message she had given the doctor. "I've just gotten off a train, and I cannot go home," she said.

Her friend immediately replied, "Can you get a cab?"

"Yes."

"Then come to my place at once. You must be nearly frozen! Are you sure you understand?"

"Yes."

Half an hour later, Esther and her husband, Ben, were at the front door of their home to welcome Ivy. They never asked any personal questions. "Do you want to stay here?" asked Esther's husband.

"If I may."

"Of course you may," said Esther.

"Certainly," said Ben.

*   *   *

Ed Bottini called every day for the next two weeks. Esther or Ben would console the concerned husband, but Ivy was unable to speak with him. Nevertheless, she was painfully aware that her inaction was causing considerable anxiety for faultless friends and family, including her eleven- and thirteen-year-old daughters, who continued to be unaware of Ivy's sexual-identity problem.

"I knew I was moving in a new direction," said Ivy, "but I didn't know how or why. I felt terribly ashamed. I was so conscious-stricken, yet I couldn't explain myself to anybody. I didn't have the confidence, knowledge, or even the technical vocabulary I felt I needed to communicate. Yet I did know how devastating the entire episode was for Eddie. I regret the pain I caused him. We never really ever discussed our separation, except in anger, because I was afraid that if I spoke to him on a rational level, I would have backed down and given in."

After a fortnight of frustration, Eddie agreed to move out of their home. He went to live with his mother, an uncomfortable arrangement that lasted until long after the snow had melted. During the same months, Ivy maintained contact with Nancy. The two women, never more than casual friends, went shopping together, and occasionally, dancing. There was nothing more to their association, which lasted until Nancy decided to go steady with another woman.

"All for the best," decided Ivy, her ardor cooled. "Besides, what have I been doing? I have two kids. My husband is out of the house and living with his mother. This is terrible!"

A reconciliation was arranged. Eddie came home, and Ivy was genuinely glad to see him. Briefly, she was able to delude herself into believing that sexual orientation can change like the weather, or be a passing diversion. But Ivy had much to learn.

"I'm glad you're home," she said to Eddie, with sincerity. Ivy loved her husband, and always would—although to this day, that statement probably is difficult for him to understand.

"Glad to be here," Eddie responded. There was little conversation. "Eddie Bottini was not a confronter, he was an avoider," Ivy explained. "For that reason, peace and tranquillity lasted longer than might be expected—until nearly summer.

In May, Nancy was again free, and telephoned. "Would you like to go dancing?" she asked, and the idea was enticing. Ivy was soon dressed and out of the house, leaving behind husband, self-recrimination, and doubts. The music Ivy heard on the dance floor had never sounded so sweet. Yet it had to end, and that evening it did, but with a difference. The highways were slick from rain, and Nancy, who was driving, lost control of the automobile. They skidded. Not only was the vehicle severely damaged, but so was Ivy's leg. As a result, it was well after midnight before Ivy, with Nancy's assistance, was finally able to limp into her house.

As they came through the door, Eddie turned off a softly playing radio and glanced at his wristwatch. He looked at the two women, saw all that he needed to see, and then turned directly to Ivy. "That's it! I'm leaving," he said. Eddie had finally lost his patience. Without further comment, he collected a few personal belongings and moved away from his wife forever.

The women's movement was another facet of Ivy's life that would not long continue. She had already come to the conclusion that the National Organization for Women was not dealing with lesbian concerns. In an attempt to rectify the situation, and to seek information for herself as well as others, Ivy convened and moderated NOW's first panel discussion on the subject Is Lesbianism a Feminist Issue? Although the question was whispered, it had never been publicly discussed. Four hundred women attended the meeting, but it would be incorrect to conclude that homosexuality was generally acceptable to NOW's membership, even to those present for the discussion.

Once Ivy became open about being a lesbian, vicious opposition developed against her position of leadership in the New York chapter of NOW. When she ran for chair of the board in 1970, tactics used against her included whispers and gutter rumors relating specifically to homosexuality. Although Ivy was elected (by a slim six votes) she felt like anything but a winner. The experience had been degrading, and people who attacked her the most venomously were people she had thought of as friends. They were the same women she had worked, argued, eaten, and marched with for the difficult years of their earliest uphill struggles. As a result of this growing homophobic animosity, Ivy resigned soon after her election.

"You've known me for four years," she told assembled members of NOW, with Irish anger in her tone of voice. "We have been like a family. You have known my dedication to the issues. Can you begin to imagine how painful this unexpected, underhanded attack has been? I am filled with dismay that many of you could be so moved by your fear of homosexuality to do the terrible things you have done, to whisper such terrible lies about me, to make those awful phone calls. It has caused a real mind shift. I sat alone in my chair at home, for days on end, trying to sort my feelings, and this is what I must say. To those of you who fabricated terrible stories, and to those

who repeated lies while knowing in your heart they were
not true, I just can't continue to associate with you. I still
have work to do, and energy to give, but there must be
a better way."

At that point Ivy departed.

Moving away from women's issues in general, she began to concentrate on lesbian issues in particular. "I had
become a knowledgeable political animal," she said.
"Working on matters concerning the school board, and
with the National Organization for Women, I had
learned that I was an effective organizer, and as a
speaker, could make a difference." Thus, with a fertile
imagination, plenty of ideas, and a growing awareness of
sensitive issues, Ivy was ready to have her say. It was then
that she toured America. Ivy's natural talent as a humor-
ist, wittily discussing women's lives and feminist issues,
brought rapid success.

However, after several years of being booked into a different city every night, after moving thousands of people
to laughter and tears, Ivy grew tired of traveling. When
in the mid-1970s she was asked to become the women's
director at Los Angeles' Gay and Lesbian Community
Services Center, she was ready for the opportunity to put
into practice ideas she had been talking about in hundreds of cities. At the same time, a hyperreligious, homophobic orange juice queen on the other side of the
continent in Florida elevated herself to infamy.

"I read everything that was written about Anita Bryant," said Ivy, "and I knew from my own experience how
dangerous such an ambitious, intolerant woman can be.
I had no illusions. And I knew that if bigoted busybodies
were already stirring up trouble for gays in Florida, then
California, if not next, would be high on their list of priorities. That's when I realized an attack upon one part of

our community is an attack against all. That's when I made a conscious decision not to work exclusively with women anymore, but to include gay men in every activity—an arrangement I hadn't pursued until Anita Bryant brought everything into perspective.

"Anita Bryant was the catalyst. She unified our commitment. Someone once said that if Anita had never existed, our gay and lesbian community would have needed to invent her, and it's true.

"We learned that our men and women must work together. The union doubles our numbers and triples our strength," concluded Ivy. "Combined efforts will always be essential if we are to succeed.

"It was together that we formed the Coalition for Human Rights—and when California Senator Briggs tried to follow in the footsteps of smiling Anita, we were ready to resist an avalanche of bigotry. My task was to join our people. Through the years, traveling, I had seen that the lesbian and gay community has tremendous diversity, including the far right and the far left—enough diversity to drive a sane person over the brink—but eventually we did all close ranks against Senator Briggs, and our enemy was overwhelmingly defeated at ballot boxes throughout the state. In the process, gay men and lesbians proved we are able to confound our enemies and celebrate our victories together. The results are dynamic.

"Now, since the defeat of Briggs' Initiative, I am totally committed to the concept of gay men and lesbians helping each other. Politically, if for no other reason, it makes good sense. Since the fight against Briggs, I've served in top leadership positions in the California Democratic party, but I want to be heard clearly on this: We can only continue to work for a political party just so long as that party responds in a meaningful way to lesbian and gay concerns. Politics is a two-way street. We refuse to be taken for granted."

On Saturday, the tenth of April 1976, an auction was held at Los Angeles' Mark IV Health Club, a bathhouse, where a handful of seminude gay slaves (all volunteers) were willingly offered for sale to nearly two hundred fifty amused and laughing male bidders. The auction was nothing more than a frivolous fund-raising event. Proceeds were designated to go to charitable and/or needy groups like HELP, Inc. (Homophile Effort for Legal Protection—an assocation that annoyed and was thoroughly despised by the police) and GLCSC (the Gay and Lesbian Community Services Center, where Ivy was still employed).

The "Great Gay Slave Auction" was not an original farce, having been produced in many lighthearted versions by numerous organizations both in and out of the homosexual community. (Nongay civic groups often "sell" skimpily veiled harem girls; high schools have annual "slave-for-a-day" events.) Nevertheless, the Los Angeles Police Department decided to take a special interest in this gay happening, and maliciously magnified its importance.

"We spent five days in consultation with the best minds of the District Attorney's and City Attorney's offices before the raid," declared Daryl F. Gates, who, at the time, was assistant to Los Angeles Chief of Police Ed Davis.

The result was an expensive, massive and foolish raid on an otherwise harmless and forgettable event. Officially designated "Operation Emancipation," the LAPD's total commitment utilized two helicopters, two well-equipped communications outposts with code names for various coordinated forces, leather costumes (with decorative chain accessories) rented from Columbia Studios, and ninety-six law enforcement personnel officially assigned to the duty—including a small army of vice officers who infiltrated and then swarmed over the bawdy auction premises.

Forty persons were arrested and carted off to jail. Some were subjected to physical abuse. Four were charged with felonies.

On being informed of the concentration of police activity in a situation where there was no public complaint, no crime, and no victims, an aide for Los Angeles City Councilwoman Peggy Stevenson described the raid as "incredible and unbelievable." Other prominent city officials wondered if the police could be so naive as to believe that their overpowering surprise attack was actually saving authentic slaves from a "fate that was worse than death."

But the gendarmerie, in the face of truth and all the evidence, were unrepentant and totally reluctant to reverse the unfortunate personal damage precipitated by their homophobic conduct. They were literally having too much fun, indiscriminately insulting gay prisoners. As a result, it was not long before those who worked in the gay community were insisting that L.A.'s "finest" clean up their act. Lesbian and gay demands were loudly seconded by Mayor Bradley's office, the City Council of Los Angeles, as well as being accompanied by an overwhelmingly positive response from major newspapers, radio, and television. Yet the result was still negative. The Los Angeles police never made any honest effort to alter their stupid behavior.

The slave auction raid made a strong impression upon Ivy Bottini. Excesses of police force in the United States had not previously seemed a pressing concern, but this blatant and unforgivable display of armed might against gay men was proof of a major homophobic illness that community-conscious lesbians knew could not be ignored. For her part, Ivy determined to be prepared when the time came to do whatever she could to alleviate an intolerable local situation.

"Why can't the police get it through their heads that they, deliberately hurting and harassing gays, are the real problem?" asked David Glascock, an openly gay deputy from the office of L.A. City Councilman Ed Edelman. Glascock added, "Some cops think it's their mission to discipline 'queers.'"

Five years later, early in 1981, there seemed to be a possibility that relations between the gay community and the Los Angeles police could be improved. Aware of the situation, Steve Schulte, executive director of the Gay and Lesbian Community Services Center, sent a personal letter to homosexual leaders and organizations who might be interested in such an endeavor. Ivy Bottini received one of Steve's letters.

The situation was simple. A large faction of the Los Angeles Police Department was, and long had been, an elite, homophobic force that arrogantly sidestepped the complaints of gay citizens. But at last, there was reason to hope for improvement because Daryl Gates, Ed Davis's successor as Los Angeles' chief of police, had made public the fact that he wanted to enter the political arena and run against Tom Bradley for the job of Mayor. To have a chance, Gates would need money, workers, and votes. In short, the talkative, ambitious, egotistical new chief of police should not continue to blatantly ignore potential voters—not even homosexuals!

Thus, what eventually was named the Gay and Lesbian Police Task Force came into existence. Ivy was chosen to be cochair along with Jim LaMaida. For Ivy it was an un-

dertaking she well understood: politics—gathering diverse community groups for a common goal—and
working as a lesbian for the benefit of gay men who,
more than women, were mistreated by police, who forget
they receive salaries from *all* taxpayers (including gays)
to "protect and serve."

After several organizational meetings of the new task
force, serious work began on the drafting of an "Agenda
for Improving Relations Between the LAPD and the Lesbian and Gay Community." It became a sophisticated list
of grievances, which was presented to Chief of Police
Gates.

Eleven points of contention were raised, and each item
was, in the best public-relations tradition, dutifully answered by Gates. He wrote, "I am aware of the fact that
discrimination for reasons of sexual orientation is a viola-
tion of the law and of public policies, and I will not tolerate any member of my Department acting contrary to
either."

A good statement.

Unfortunately, Gates also said for publication at a later
date, "Who would want to work with one?"—meaning
gays and lesbians. They are "unnatural," he said, and he
stated that any recruiting of gay and lesbian police officers (which had finally become standard practice in San
Francisco) would be "over my dead body!"

Daryl Gates did not prove to be an adept politician.
Conflicting statements were his undoing, and he did not
become mayor. Nevertheless, Gates' political ambitions
were the basis for one small step forward made by the
gay community. The eleventh and final item on the
"Agenda for Improving Relations" had asked for the
chief of police's support in the creation of a citizens' police advisory committee selected from the gay and lesbian

community. To that request, Gates had responded, "I am sure there is much yet to be done before suspicion and distrust on both sides can be totally eliminated. Even if that can never be, it is certainly a worthwhile goal to pursue. You may rest assured that this Department will not abandon that objective." The Gay and Lesbian Police Task Force has been unable to hold the chief to that statement.

"Working with Gates' police department was like running our heads into a brick building," admitted Ivy. "We were stonewalled. The police would soft-talk us a lot and be polite. We'd make complaints, and they would say, 'We'll look into it.' But there wasn't any progress.

"My co-chair and I actually got an appointment to go into Gates' inner sanctum, where we chatted with him. It was a congenial morning. He was nice. We were nice. We talked about our community and our complaints. He talked about horses. At the end of the session, as members of a task force, we figured working through the Police Commission, a civilian board with considerable power, had to be better than having the chief of police smile us out of existence."

On April 14, 1982, the Gay and Lesbian Police Advisory Task Force was officially recognized by the Los Angeles Police Commission. "Theoretically, that move was supported by Chief Gates, but in actuality, I think it blew his mind," said Ivy. "I doubt that he thought it would ever happen.

"The minds of many police still have not changed. They would have us believe they're unable to correct the antigay attitudes that some of their people display on the street. I think, as an official policy, they tell their men and women to treat everybody alike, but for some reason they don't seem able to implement the concept. Sometimes a recruit with an open mind gets hooked up to an older, not wiser, cop who nurtures an ingrained hatred for gay men or lesbians. Soon the impressionable kid is thinking and acting the same way. What can you do? Since their salaries are paid by our taxes, they must be dense not to figure out why, election after election, we who feel betrayed refuse to vote them an increase of funds.

"At least new law enforcement priorities have evolved, but only because when Burt Pines was District Attorney, he refused to prosecute homosexuals who never should have been arrested in the first place. That was a powerful influence.

"Even the rotten apples on the force now know they have to work with the gay and lesbian community," said Ivy, smiling, "The police realize they can no longer just pick us up and throw us in jail. And that is progress!

"There is some semblance of justice for us. Not all the time. Far from it. Plenty of work remains. But we have a shot at justice. And although there have been defeats and setbacks, more often these days, justice prevails.

"We know from extensive scientific research that at least ten percent of the world's population consists of gay men and lesbians. In North America, in 1980, that computed to be something in excess of thirty-one million—thirty-one million!!!—breathing, working, loving homosexuals. Doesn't that stretch your imagination? Especially if there once was a time you thought you were the only 'queer' person that ever lived?

"Many of us are working to make this a better life for people we love, and for an infinity of generations to follow. If you're in the closet, why not give serious thought to coming out and giving us a hand? Nobody can tell you there is no risk, but you'll probably feel healthier, considerably more honest, and a whole lot happier."

Epilogue

After fifteen years of heated and repeated rejection, New York City's Gay Rights Bill was finally passed into law on the twentieth of March 1986. Approval was overwhelming, in no small part because New York's Mayor, who vigorously supported the bill, had made a deal with the City Council.

A few weeks later, when asked to sign an amendment that would have diminished the scope of the progay and lesbian legislation, Mayor Koch braved the displeasure of politicians, and declined. It was only the fifth time during his long tenure in office that Koch had used the veto.

"Rather than step back from full protection of their rights," said the Mayor, "I would ask the council to trust the capacity for understanding and tolerance present in all New Yorkers."

Representative Barney Frank, Massachusetts' popular United States Congressman, publicly revealed his homosexuality by intentionally giving that personal information to an inquiring newspaper reporter. On May 30, 1987, when Frank's story broke on the front page of *The Boston Globe*, response from his constituents was favorable—at a ratio of six to one.

In an interview the following Tuesday, Representative Frank said, "I have no reason to expect anyone to be reading my obituary anytime soon, but I do fly home on weekends, and we can all be hit by a truck, and I don't want the focus to be: Was he or wasn't he? Did he or didn't he? The inference would be that I'm ashamed, when I'm not!"

Three years later, in 1990, following a heart attack and an overblown sex scandal, Barney Frank once again was easily reelected to the United States Congress, together with another openly gay legislator from Massachusetts, Gerry Studds. Representative Studds has been successful in combating entrenched military bigotry, forcing full release of a now famous Department of Defense study which acknowledges that gays and lesbians actually make better than average members of the armed forces.

A reasonable estimate is that fifty-four thousand unidentified gay men and lesbians distinguished themselves as officers and enlisted personnel in the 1991 air, sea, and ground war that stretched from Saudi Arabia across Kuwait and into Iraq. That information, however, should not delude anyone into believing that the American military will not at its convenience unceremoniously dump suspected homosexuals whenever their contributions are not required.

"Every report the military has commissioned since World War II says there is no reason gays cannot serve in the military," declares Sergeant First Class Perry Watkins, who retired at the conclusion of 1990. "There is only an inaccurate perception that there's a problem. It's a ludicrous argument."

Watkins is a black man who enlisted in the Army in 1967. He marked "Yes" on his original enlistment questionnaire, which asked if he was homosexual—and, as an openly gay person, reenlisted three times. After many years, the Army arbitrarily decided to rid itself of Watkins, but Watkins countered with a successful lawsuit.

After an appeal to the U.S. Supreme Court in 1990, the reluctant Army was finally forced to promote Watkins and to give him his back pay and his pension.

Sergeant Watkins is the only openly gay individual known to successfully complete an Army career and retire with benefits. His advice to any gay person enlisting or drafted is to inform the military in writing that he or she is homosexual. Watkins counsels that the individual, for his or her future security in any branch of the armed forces, must declare from the beginning, "I'm gay. If you want me, take me as I am." Continuing the advice, Sergeant Watkins declares, "If they say no, remember that you as a person are very valuable."

In 1975, would-be employees of Pacific Bell filed a lawsuit against that telephone company because it used the notation "Code 48" to identify lesbians and gay men on its application files—as part of a policy of job discrimination. Four years later, in 1979, as a result of related appeals, California Supreme Court Justice Matthew O. Tobriner delivered the court's majority opinion in which he stated that disclosure of an individual's sexual orientation is a "political act" entitled to protection under the law.

"One important aspect of the struggle for equal rights," wrote Justice Tobriner, "is to induce homosexual individuals to 'come out of the closet,' acknowledge their sexual preferences, and to associate with others in working for equal rights."

Eleven years after the filing of the lawsuit against Pacific Bell—on December 4, 1986—representatives of the huge business met with gay activists to announce that the telephone company would settle out of court, having agreed to pay $2 million in costs, plus a $3 million penalty to an estimated two hundred fifty persons who were denied either jobs or promotions between 1970 and 1980 because of being homosexual.

Women, blacks, and other activists have learned that the filing of lawsuits is most often the only method of achieving equal rights and the fundamentals of life and liberty that many nongay white men take for granted. A great variety of civil cases dealing with issues vital to the lesbian and gay community continually work their way through American courts.

Joseph Steffan, a cadet battalion commander with an outstanding four-year academic record at the Naval Academy at Annapolis, was forced to resign two months before his graduation. Separation was based upon Steffan's admission of being homosexual rather than on any evidence of misconduct. The lawsuit filed by Steffan and the Lambda Legal Defense and Education Fund which represents him asks, among other considerations, that the court issue a statement that the U.S. Department of Defense's refusal to employ declared lesbians and gays in military service is unconstitutional.

On the West Coast, Mitchell Grobeson, a homosexual sergeant in the Los Angeles Police Department who served from 1981 until 1988 and received well over a hundred commendations for service, explains that once he was suspected of being gay, frequent harassment, a conspiratorial lack of backup in dangerous patrol situations, and death threats from homophobic officers forced him to resign. Grobeson's lawsuit, supported by the American Civil Liberties Union, seeks an official reversal of the Los Angeles Police Department's unwholesome attitude toward its undeclared homosexual officers and an end to the well-publicized mistreatment of civilian members of the gay and lesbian community.

Also in court during 1991 was FBI agent Frank Buttino, once a highly regarded leader with the FBI who directed numerous major cases, including the notorious
Patty Hearst kidnapping. Despite an illustrious career,
Buttino was summarily fired after admitting his homosexuality. If successful, Buttino's lawsuit against the FBI will
help to terminate the agency's irrational refusal to employ acknowledged gays and lesbians—a ban dictated,
strangely enough, by legendary director of the FBI J. Ed-
gar Hoover, himself a confirmed bachelor whose sex life
was only discussed in whispers.

When Gay Pride Day was celebrated on June 28, 1987,
for the eighteenth consecutive year, there were parades
in major cities including Boston, Chicago, Houston, Los
Angeles, Louisville, New York, San Francisco, and Seattle. Tourists and heterosexual spectators seemed less
shocked or offended than in previous years by the public
appearance of marching homosexuals.

In New York City, tens of thousands of gay men and
women walked past hundreds of thousands of people
who watched from windows and sidewalks. Included in
the parade ranks were twenty-four police officers who,
for the first time, stepped smartly beneath their own banner, which identified them as the GAY OFFICERS ACTION
LEAGUE.

When the homosexual police marched past the steps of
St. Patrick's Cathedral, a rowdy religious group displayed
placards that read DEPORT GAYS. Later, speaking of the
small band of antigay demonstrators who were present
during the parade, one gay policeman said, "They have a
constitutional right not to like us—and we'll support that
right!"

Less tolerant, officials of Manhattan's 1991 Saint Patrick's Day Parade tried to prevent a hundred and thirty-five member Irish gay group from participating in the march. As a result of this discrimination, New York's Mayor David Dinkins threatened to boycott the annual event. When a compromise was reached, lesbians and gay men were invited to march with one division of Manhattan's chapter of the Ancient Order of Hibernians; and Mayor Dinkins gave up his traditional place at the head of the parade to march with them.

More than two million spectators watched the celebration and not all were friendly. Supercilious officials on the reviewing stand turned their chubby behinds toward the Mayor and the gays as they passed, but Dinkins was undaunted. "Every time I heard someone boo," the Mayor said later, "it strengthened my resolve that it was the right thing to do."

Jimmy Swaggart, Jerry Falwell, and Rex Humbard are television preachers who were listed as directors of the American Coalition for Traditional Values that sent California State Senator Ed Davis a letter signed by Reverend Tim LaHaye, chairman of the group. The letter solicited Senator Davis to reject any support from gay organizations because, said the letter, homosexuals spread AIDS and violate "traditional family values."

For his reply, Davis (in a neat turnabout from the ten years, 1969 to 1978, when he was Los Angeles' homophobic chief of police) wrote: "Dr. LaHaye, I can only interpret your letter as an attempt to deprive some of our citizens of one of our most fundamental and cherished rights—the right to participate in the electoral process. . . .

"By even suggesting the abridgment of anyone's constitutional rights, you lost whatever presumptuous claim you may have had to speak for traditional values . . . and you certainly do not speak for conservatives. . . .

"I close this letter by asking you to read two short documents with which you may not be familiar: the Declaration of Independence and the Bill of Rights."

The Christian Science Monitor reported on June 21, 1985, that New York, New Mexico, and the District of Columbia had passed laws which state that homosexuality is not sufficient cause to disqualify persons from adopting or giving foster care to children. Six additional states—California, Missouri, Oregon, South Carolina, Washington, and Wisconsin—were following similar, but unwritten, guidelines. Nevertheless, in many states emotional bias still replaces reason if young people are involved.

Until recently, Florida laws totally prohibited the adoption or foster placement of any child into a gay home. An exception to the rule occurred with the birth of two black girls who had inherited AIDS. No person of the heterosexual multitude was interested in taking the unfortunate babies into their homes. But suddenly, in Lakeland, Florida, it was "just fine" for two white lesbians—Reverend Mary Marriman of Metropolitan Community Church and her lover—to house, care for, and cherish the children who were shunned by others.

Some of those same nongay Florida residents had in the past been quick to join Anita Bryant's so-called crusade, and quick to condemn homosexuals by mouthing Anita's hypocritical slogan "Save the children," but when actually given such an opportunity, they clearly demonstrated how little genuine interest they had in children's welfare. Instead, it was two gay women who proved to be courageous and compassionate.

In years past, judges in custody cases automatically ruled against the homosexual parent when one parent was homosexual and the other was not. No longer is that always true. An increasing number of gay women and men are fighting for nondiscriminatory custody of their own children—and winning.

Craig Corbett of Palm Springs, California, was already a conscientious stepfather when his lover, Frank Batey, died. Frank's survivors were Corbett and Frank's sixteen-year-old heterosexual son, Brian Batey, who had previously observed and rejected religious homophobia to which his mother had exposed him. Corbett was successful in his effort to be named Brian's temporary guardian (Brian's stated preference), and in a San Diego closed court hearing, Corbett was awarded custody on July 8, 1987. The loser was Mrs. Betty Lou Batey, who more than once had flagrantly violated court orders concerning visitation and custody. Mrs. Batey, a Pentecostalist, had received backing in court from Concerned Women for America (a fundamentalist group), which supplied lawyers for the unsuccessful custody fight.

Similar disputes are increasingly being judged on merit, not sexuality, in courts today. And very much to the point, as reported in *The New York Times* on January 21, 1987, is the work of Dr. Robert J. Howell, professor of clinical psychology at Brigham Young University. After an extensive survey of seventeen scientific projects studying children who live with homosexual parents, Dr. Howell concluded that "while custody decisions have tended to reflect stereotyped beliefs or fears concerning the detrimental effects of homosexual parenting practices on child development, a review of the research consistently fails to document any evidence substantiating those fears."

Not only has the nurturing of children by gay people met with heterosexual disapproval, but adult gay relationships, one-to-one, have also faced unreasonable barriers. Antigay individuals and organizations have long condemned the homosexual community for its apparent sexual promiscuity while at the very same time (ignoring the inconsistency of their position) they have been emphatic that permanent gay and lesbian unions must not be validated. At least one small legislative step toward ending that vacuous dichotomy was implemented on Valentine's Day, 1991, when the city clerk's office in San Francisco began issuing certificates of domestic partnership. Two hundred fifty pairs, mostly same-sex couples, immediately took advantage of the new law. In ceremonies held the same day, certificate recipients wore corsages and boutonnieres, had rice thrown over them, and posed for photographs. One of the men involved, Larry Brinkin of San Francisco's Human Relations Commission, stated, "We still won't have the benefits that married couples have, but that can't subtract from the joy I feel inside."

On an international note, October 1990 marked the first full year in which homosexual marriages have been legal in progressive Denmark. During those first twelve months approximately 575 male couples and 125 female couples were wed. Two divorces are reported.

Not all stories end with a smile. We choose to close with an important, somewhat different slice of history.

On the third of August 1982, a police officer went to the Georgia home of Michael Hardwick to serve a warrant for nonpayment of a minor fine. A man answered the door, gave the policeman permission to enter, and instructed him, if he so desired, to walk down a hallway to Hardwick's bedroom. There, with its door ajar, the officer discovered twenty-nine-year-old Michael with another man. The two were clearly visible, engaged in oral sex—which, under the misleading label of "sodomy," has been a felony in Georgia since 1816.

Both men were arrested.

However, District Attorney Lewis Slaton dropped the charges when the case was bound over to a superior court in Fulton County—although there was nothing to prevent the charge of sodomy against Michael from being reinstituted at any time during a period of years prescribed by the state's statute of limitations. "That," said Kathy Wilde, Hardwick's attorney, "was the point at which he decided to challenge the law."

In May of 1985, the United States Court of Appeals for the Eleventh Circuit decided that Georgia's law against sodomy was unconstitutional. As a part of its ruling, the three-judge court wrote, "The Constitution prevents the states from unduly interfering in certain individual decisions critical to personal autonomy because those decisions are essentially private and beyond the reach of a civilized society."

That was good news for the national gay community, but celebrations were premature. Georgia officials decided to make an appeal—which the highest court in the land agreed to hear. Georgia claimed that its sodomy statute—which in practice was not applied to heterosexuals—prevented "unnatural acts which are crimes against the laws of man and God."

On June 30, 1986, the Supreme Court of the United States, by a close vote of 5 to 4, reached its surprising decision. The majority opinion declared that homosexual claims for a constitutional right to engage in private sex acts are "insupportable" and "facetious."

It was a dark night—not only for homosexuals, but for all Americans who understand and fight for the fragile concepts of our precious liberty.

In his eloquent dissenting opinion, United States Supreme Court Justice Harry A. Blackmun wrote, "This case is about 'the most comprehensive of rights, and the right most valued by civilized men,' namely 'the right to be let alone.' . . .

"The fact that individuals define themselves in a significant way through their intimate sexual relationships with others suggests, in a nation as diverse as ours, that there may be many 'right' ways of conducting those relationships, and that much of the richness of a relationship will come from the freedom an individual has to choose the form and nature of these intensely personal bonds. . . .

"The right of an individual to conduct intimate relationships in the intimacy of his or her own home seems to me to be the heart of the Constitution's protection of privacy. . . .

"That certain, but by no means all, religious groups condemn the behavior at issue gives the State no license to impose their judgments on the entire citizenry. The legitimacy of secular legislation depends instead on whether the State can advance some justification for its law beyond its conformity to religious doctrine. Thus, far from buttressing his case, petitioner's invocation of Leviticus, Romans, St. Thomas Aquinas, and sodomy's heretical status during the Middle Ages, undermines his suggestion that [the Georgia Code] represents a legitimate use of secular coercive power. A state can no more punish private behavior because of religious intolerance than it can punish such behavior because of racial animus. . . .

"This case involves no real interference with the rights of others, for the mere knowledge that other individuals do not adhere to one's value system cannot be a legally cognizable interest, let alone an interest that can justify invading the houses, hearts, and minds of citizens who choose to live their lives differently."

In an editorial printed two days later, *The Los Angeles Times* took the position that "The rigid and hostile attitude woven through White's (majority) opinion will discourage those not inclined to sit in righteous judgment of others, but they can hope, with Blackmun, 'that the court soon will reconsider its analysis and conclude that depriving individuals of the right to choose for themselves how to conduct their intimate relationships poses a far greater threat to the values most deeply rooted in our nation's history than tolerance of nonconformity could ever do.'"

For those of us who are out in the gay and lesbian community, there can never be retreat. It is our intention to continue our loving relationships no matter what any court may say. We will continue to defend our country in all ways, including service in the armed forces. We will not rest until a National Gay Rights Bill is passed and signed into law. Nor will we permit any individual or group to stop us from working and enjoying our lives wherever love and honor are most bright.

This book ends, but courage will continue.

Reverend Troy D. Perry
Thomas L. P. Swicegood

THOMAS SWICEGOOD

Reverend Troy D. Perry

Reverend Perry and Tom Swicegood have been friends since 1970, when Tom walked into church services at Hollywood's Encore Theater and asked for permission to write a book about Troy Perry and the church he founded on October 6, 1968. Troy was born in North Florida and grew up with his mother, four brothers, and many Baptist and Pentacostal relatives. After Army duty in Germany, Troy returned to the United States, where he became a Church of God preacher, married, fathered two sons, was excommunicated twice, and divorced. He has been a leader in gay and lesbian political struggles and is the founder and moderator of the Universal Fellowship of Metropolitan Community Churches.

Thomas L. P. Swicegood

Born in Key West, Tom Swicegood attended St. Petersburg's Admiral Farragut Academy and was graduated from the University of Florida. He served during the Korean War as deck officer on the *Storis*, a Coast Guard icebreaker in Alaska; and in the eastern Mediterranean was first lieutenant on USCGC *Courier*, a unique vessel broadcasting Voice of America programs into Arab and Iron Curtain countries. Tom has hitchhiked on military aircraft across Europe, Africa, Asia, and the Pacific; spent months photographing the U.S.S.R and China; has written for television; worked for CBS in Washington, D.C.; and is author, producer, and director of feature motion pictures.